# A CASEBOOK ON

# Ezra Pound

Edited by **WILLIAM VAN O'CONNOR**

University of Minnesota

and **EDWARD STONE**

Ohio University

THOMAS Y. CROWELL COMPANY, NEW YORK    ESTABLISHED 1834

Library of Congress Catalog Card Number 59–9400

Manufactured in the United States of America
By the Cornwall Press, Inc., Cornwall, N.Y.

for
W. V., E. L., and J. M.
and
Donald and Ella Selvage

# Acknowledgments

The editors want to thank the authors and editors who gave us permission to use the articles in this volume. Also we wish to thank Miss Catherine Nelson of the Ohio University Library and Mrs. Margaret Sant Ambrogio of Athens, Ohio, for their help in assembling the materials of this volume and in preparing the copy, respectively, and Mr. H. A. Sieber, formerly of the Library of Congress, for judicious and helpful advice at several points. Lastly, we want to thank Philip Winsor, of the Thomas Y. Crowell Company, for his many contributions, not a few of them well beyond the call of ordinary duty.

William Van O'Connor
Edward Stone

# Contents

# Introduction

Ezra Pound is a controversial figure. As a young man he helped
to formulate the break with Victorian literary standards. He was
generous with his time and energies, helping poets like Eliot and
Frost to get into print and Joyce to find a publisher for *Ulysses*.
Many writers, including Yeats and Hemingway, have acknowledged
their debt to him. But Pound was never one to speak softly or to
understate a criticism—and there were many literary men as well
as readers who objected to his brashness. Others objected to his
poetic experiments, especially in the *Cantos*. There can be no debate however about his having been an important innovator in
modern literature.

During World War II, Pound broadcast from Rome, addressing
himself to American audiences, including American troops. He
talked about many subjects, including his own poetry, but he was
especially concerned with certain monetary theories. He deplored
the war between Italy and the U.S. The U.S. government indicted
him for acts of treason, and he was eventually flown to Washington
to stand trial. But a board of psychiatrists declared him insane and
unfit to stand trial. He was committed to St. Elizabeth's Hospital,
where he remained for twelve years.

At Pisa, where he had been held by the American Army, he had
written more cantos. They were published as *The Pisan Cantos*. The
volume won the Bollingen Award, sponsored by the Library of
Congress. A vigorous controversy, involving many writers, editors,
and magazines, ensued. Eventually the controversy died down—

1

but even now tempers are likely to flare during discussions of Pound or of the Bollingen Award for *The Pisan Cantos.*

During his stay at St. Elizabeth's, Pound continued to write and to publish. He was also associated with John Kasper and others who have been accused of holding racist theories and of fomenting race hatred. At fairly regular intervals friends of Pound urged his release, saying he would never be tried, since the psychiatrists said he was incurable, and that his continued confinement was, in effect, life imprisonment of a person who must always be presumed innocent under the law, and therefore cruel and inhuman punishment. Eventually the U.S. District Court dropped the indictment at the request of the U.S. District Attorney, and he was released. He accompanied his wife to Italy to live with his daughter.

The articles in *A Casebook on Ezra Pound* discuss various parts of his career, implications of the Bollingen Award, and our government's treatment of Pound. There are samples of Pound's cantos, and excerpts from his broadcasts. And there is a long bibliography of books by Pound and of books and articles about him.

In the exercises, the student will find suggestions for short and long term papers. He should be able to write these after reading and studying the materials he finds in *A Casebook.* He will also find a few library exercises. If the instructor wishes he can assign other topics which will involve using not only *A Casebook* but some of the articles and books listed in the bibliography.

*The Medical, Legal, Literary and Political Status of Ezra Weston [Loomis] Pound [1885-     ], Selected Facts and Comments* by H. A. Sieber, The Library of Congress Legislative Reference Service, March 31, 1958, revised April 14, 1958.

# Citation with Honorary Degree from Hamilton College

Ezra Pound: native of Idaho, graduate of Hamilton College in the class of 1905, poet, critic, and prose writer of great distinction. Since completing your college career you have had a life full of significance in the arts. You have found that you could work more happily in Europe than in America and so have lived most of the past 30 years an expatriate making your home in England, France, and Italy, but your writings are known wherever English is read. Your feet have trodden paths, however, where the great reading public could give you few followers—into Provençal and Italian poetry, into Anglo-Saxon and Chinese. From all of these excursions you have brought back treasure. Your translations from the Chinese have, for example, led one of the most gifted of contemporary poets to call you the inventor of Chinese poetry of our time. Your Alma Mater, however, is an old lady who has not always understood where you were going, but she has watched you with interest and pride if not always with understanding. The larger public has also been at times amazed at your political and economic as well as your artistic credo, and you have retaliated by making yourself—not unintentionally perhaps—their gadfly. Your range of interests is immense, and whether or not your theories of society survive, your name is permanently linked with the development of English poetry in the 20th century. *Your reputation is international, you have guided many poets into new paths, you have pointed new directions, and the historian of the future in tracing the development of your growing mind will inevitably, we are happy*

3

*to think, be led to Hamilton and to the influence of your college teachers.* You have ever been a generous champion of younger writers as well as artists in other fields, and for this fine and rare human quality and for your own achievements in poetry and prose, we honor you.

Nathaniel Weyl, *Treason,*
(Washington: Public Affairs Press, 1950)

# The Strange Case of Ezra Pound

by NATHANIEL WEYL

"I could never take him as a steady diet. Never. He was often brilliant, but an ass. But I never . . . ceased to love him."
—William Carlos Williams on Ezra Pound.

"He is abnormally grandiose, is expansive and exuberant in manner, exhibiting pressure of speech, discursiveness and distractibility. . . . He is, in other words, insane. . . ."
—Report of four alienists to Justice Bolitha J. Laws concerning Ezra Pound.

On November 18, 1945, a man of sixty with unruly, graying hair and a stubble beard (which had once come to a fine Mandarin point) was removed from an Army plane and taken to the District of Columbia jail. The passenger was Ezra Loomis Pound, born in a pioneer's cabin in Hailey, Idaho. A distinguished critic, a revolutionist in poetry, a man of sprawling scholarship and subtle cadences, of lucid images and maundering hallucinations, he had at last come home to his native land. He had come home to stand trial for having betrayed it.

When he was arrested near Genoa in the springtime of 1945, Ezra Pound made a statement that was characteristic:

"If I ain't worth more alive than dead, that's that. If a man isn't willing to take some risk for his opinions, either his opinions are no good or he's no good."

5

A man going on trial for his life on a political charge should be buoyed by the belief that he stands for some general idea of principle. Here was Pound, the putative wizard of words and cadences, striving to hit a colloquial note and sounding as off-key as a high-school band grappling with a Beethoven symphony. To grasp the difference, compare Pound's political testament with almost anything John Brown had to say when on trial for his life.

Ezra Pound was the only American radio traitor who formed more than a ripple in the tidal stream of Western culture. His creative and critical work has constituted a contribution of undeniable consequence to that stream. He understood and had once spoken the common tongue of civilized man—and yet he had betrayed his birthright and deliberately merged with forces of nihilism. Pound's fellow workers in the field of radio treason had been the pygmies, the simians, the mercenaries and the frustrates found by the fascists in the backwash of Western culture. Surely, there must have been moments when Ezra Pound realized that he was keeping incongruous company.

To the intellectuals, Pound's betrayal seemed infinitely more heinous than that of the others. One expects little from an animal, but much from a man. The intellectuals were not emotionally interested in the fate of a street ruffian, such as Joe McWilliams, the Yorkville storm trooper. They could follow the trial of Mildred Gillars with a diluted sense of compassion. The psychoneurotic failures like Best and Chandler aroused no strong reactions of either pity or revulsion.

But precisely because he retained some of his standards of intelligent speech, Pound was the most guarded, unemotional and ineffective of all of America's radio traitors. To those who recall the almost unbearable tension of the blood-soaked Italian front, it will seem incredible that any of Pound's queries or metaphors could have induced American soldiers to throw down their rifles and surrender.

## THE FUGITIVE

Pound's entire life was a flight from the soil that had nurtured him. In college, he read world literature omnivorously and issued himself a party card in the American aristocracy of intellect. He was both shy and domineering. William Carlos Williams recollects how he would read his poetry—his voice trailing off into inaudibility. Pound was so unsure of himself that he once asked for male reinforcement in a tactical operation which, by its very nature, must be done alone—that of picking up a girl, *one* girl, Williams emphasizes. And even so, he botched it.

Shortly after Ehrlich discovered the "magic bullet"—606— Pound wanted to take Williams with him to the North Coast of Africa. He thought there were enough syphilitic chieftains there so that they could both make a fortune and retire within a year to write poetry. Nothing came of the scheme.

Shortly after being given a position on the faculty of Wabash College, he was discharged for being "the Latin Quarter type"; thereafter, all academic doors in the United States slammed in his face. At twenty-three, he was in London and had published *Personae*—a work described by Edward Thomas as replete with "the beauty of passion, sincerity and intensity, not of beautiful words and images and suggestions."

Pound was a constructive iconoclast. His "great contribution to the work of other poets," T. S. Eliot once said, ". . . is his insistence upon the immensity of the amount of *conscious* labor to be performed by the poet; and his invaluable suggestions for the kind of training the poet should give himself—study of form, metric and vocabulary in the poetry of divers literature, and study of good prose."

Preoccupied with the language as music and with the subtlest tonal patterns which could be constructed with it, Pound advised the young poet to "fill his mind with the finest cadences he can discover, preferably in a foreign language so that the meaning of the words may be less likely to divert his attention from the movement; e.g. Saxon charms, Hebridean folk songs, the verse of Dante, and the lyrics of Shakespeare—if he can dissociate the vocabulary from the cadence."

His emphasis on poetry as cadence and pure music induced him to write verse which was a mélange of snatches from living and dead tongues, incomprehensible to all but an eclectic minority. A dilettante student of the Chinese written language, Pound was entranced with the ideogram and experimented with the instantaneous presentation of complex thought in an ultimate of compactness. This resulted often enough in "intellectualized chop suey," or, more accurately, in the reduction of poetry to cryptograms,—the deciphering of which was an arduous mental process wherein the emotional reactions of the reader were inevitably deadened.

Needless to say, Pound was an esoteric and a starving one at that. The young Pound of London and the Latin Quarter was the very model of a Bohemian. His beard was bright red and stiletto pointed. His hair was a lion's mane, his collars Byronic and his cape long and flowing. He was a rootless tumbleweed on the earth's surface.

About 1915, T. S. Eliot writes, Pound "was living in a small dark flat in Kensington. In the largest room he cooked, by artificial light; in the lightest but smallest room, which was inconveniently triangular, he did his work and received his visitors. There he lived until he moved, in 1922, I think, to Paris; but he seemed always to be only a temporary squatter. This appearance was due, not only to his restless energy—in which it was difficult to distinguish the energy from the restlessness and fidgets, so that every room, even a big one, seemed too small for him—but to a kind of resistance against growing into any environment. In America, he would no doubt have always seemed on the point of going abroad; in London, he always seemed on the point of crossing the Channel. I have never known a man, of any nationality, to live so long out of his native country without seeming to settle anywhere else."

His most salient characteristic was an Olympian arrogance and an urge to master others. Even the loyal T. S. Eliot describes him as "a dominating director," adding: "No one could have been kinder to younger men, or to writers who, whether younger or not, seemed to him worthy and unrecognized . . . He liked to be the impresario for younger men, as well as the animator of artistic activity in any milieu in which he found himself. In this role he would go to any lengths of generosity and kindness; from inviting constantly to dinner a struggling author whom he suspected of being underfed, of giving away clothing (though his shoes and underwear were almost the only garments which resembled those of other men sufficiently to be worn by them), to trying to find jobs, collect subsidies, get work published and then get it criticized and praised."

Pound "always had a passion to teach." A perfectionist, he regarded his protégés impersonally "as art or literature machines to
be carefully tended and oiled, for the sake of their potential output." The obvious corollary which Eliot drew was: "Pound
was always a masterly judge of poetry; a more fallible judge, I
think, of men." He was also a perfectionist and unwilling to brook
anything which he thought smacked of mediocrity. He had a com-
pelling desire to be the Dalai Lama of all poets.

This not unsympathetic portrayal is the work of a colleague and
disciple, who shared Pound's strong antipathy toward American
democracy. It was written at a time when Pound faced possible
death as a traitor. Another poet, William Carlos Williams, sketched
Pound's countenance with harsher lines.

"Ezra always insisted in the loudest terms," Williams writes,
"on the brilliance and profundity of his mind. He doesn't have a
great mind and never did but that doesn't make him any the less
a good poet. His stupidities coupled with his overweening self
esteem have brought him down. . . ." Pound had "the most acute
ear for metrical sequences, to the point of genius, that we have
ever known," but he was also—Williams said forthrightly—"the
biggest damn fool and faker in the business."

Where T. S. Eliot speaks of Pound's incredible self-discipline
and vast capacity for work (he had turned out twenty books by
the time he was forty) Williams calls him "a lazy animal in many
ways."

Although a close friend of his at the time, Williams was irritated
at the way Ezra Pound would always walk one pace ahead of his
companions. He commented: "I remember my brother once in
the same situation turned and walked off in the opposite direction."


## WANDERINGS OF AN EXPATRIATE

Ezra Pound was for a long time one of the awe-inspiring figures
of the Left Bank. Ernest Hemingway, James Joyce, Gertrude Stein
and Ezra Pound were the four towering leaders of the Paris expatriate band of literary iconoclasts. Pound turned out massive
works of criticism, creation and translation: the *Propertius,* the

*Cantos,* renditions of Chinese literature, appraisals of the troubadours and of Japanese drama. "Thus, year after year, since the appearance of the *Personae,*" Charles Norman writes, "Pound has brought forth a body of literature without parallel in our time, a mass of work which has inspired other writers and helped to shape their styles; and he did this without much encouragement from critics in the United States and on an income which few would have been content to struggle with."

Unfortunately, there is no place in our economic system for a writers' writer, particularly if he happens to be a path-breaker in poetry. The successful writers are conformists who have no reason to subsidize literary revolutions; the others find it hard enough to support themselves.

Pound was never too busy or too poor to take up the battleaxe in defense of any powerful writing which fell dead from the presses. He championed Rabindranath Tagore and Richard Aldington. When a Paris crowd howled down the unconventional *Ballet Mecanique* of George Antheil, Pound wrote a book in defense of the composer. Though intellectually an anti-semite, Ezra Pound sang the praises of Heinrich Heine and dedicated his *Culture* to the poet, Louis Zukofsky. And when he was on trial for treason, the Jewish poet whom he had befriended wrote:

"I never felt the least trace of anti-semitism in his presence. Nothing he ever said to me made me feel the embarrassment I always have for the 'Goy' in whom a residue of antagonism to 'Jew' remains. If we had occasion to use the word 'Jew' and 'Goy' they were no more or less ethnological in their sense than 'Chinese' and 'Italian.' "

At first, Ezra Pound was an expatriate only in the physical sense. When Harriet Monroe founded the important magazine, *Poetry,* Pound wrote her a long letter:

"Are you for American poetry or for poetry? The latter is more important, but it is important that America should boost the former, provided it don't mean a blindness to the art. The glory of any nation is to produce art that can be exported without disgrace to its origin." He appendaged this note, written in the summer of 1912:

"P.S. Any agonizing that tends to hurry what I believe in the end to be inevitable, our American Risorgimento, is dear to me. That awakening will make the Italian Renaissance look like a tempest in a teapot! The force we have, and the impulse, but the guiding sense, the discrimination in applying the force, we must wait and strive for."

Miss Monroe appointed Pound as an unpaid foreign editor of her magazine. The relationship was reminiscent of that Greek philosopher, captured in war and sold into bondage, who auctioned himself off on the slave market with the dry: "Is there any man here who wants to buy a master?"

As Miss Monroe recalls their collaboration: "Thus began the rather violent, but on the whole salutary, discipline under the lash of which the editor of the new magazine felt herself being rapidly educated, while all incrustations of habit and prejudice were ruthlessly swept away. Ezra Pound was born to be a great teacher. The American universities, which, at this time of his developing strength, failed, one and all, to install him as the head of an English department, missed a dynamic influence which would have been felt wherever English writing is taught. It is not entirely his fault if he has become somewhat embittered . . ."

In the middle twenties, Pound went to Rapallo, Italy, withdrawing from the world of the cafés. He read medieval manuscripts, and, when the depression came, began to pore over economic theories. The reasons for this decisive flight into solitude remain obscure and debatable. Among them surely were his poverty and rejection by his native land. Was he, as William Carlos Williams suggests, a giant in the creation of aesthetic form, lacking a content, or unifying force, with which to fill it? In plainer language was "the thing that finally ruined Ezra" nothing less than "plain emptiness?" J. V. Healy puts the same idea somewhat more tactfully when he remarks: ". . . Eliot's success and Pound's failure lay mostly in Eliot's possession of a synthesizing imagination and Pound's lack of one."

Under more favorable circumstances, Pound might have become a comparatively prosperous poet who resided in America, but he could never have become a poet of America in the sense that Walt Whitman was. He scorned the values of democracy, the discipline of science, the faith in technology and blunt tool of pragmatism. He had removed himself progressively from the American scene to the outmost limits of time and space. Other eminent Americans ultimately rejected American values—notably Henry James and Henry Adams—but none of them became traitors.

"Ezra is one of a well recognized group of Americans who can't take the democratic virus and stand up under it," Williams comments.

### MONETARY ECONOMIST

Pound was soon dating his letters to American friends from Rapallo according to the calendar of the fascist revolution. He published a book on economics with a postscript signed: *E. P., Feb. 12, anno XII dell' era Fascista.* He had apparently been abroad long enough to forget that February 12th was Lincoln's birthday.

The Great Depression had come and Pound, along with many others, pondered over the fact that millions were idle and hungry while the machines that could clothe them and the farms that could feed them gathered dust and grew weeds.

In search for a solution, he turned his mind to the discipline of economics, and shortly found his economic Koran in the writings of one Silvio Gesell (1862-1930). To all respectable economists, Gesell seemed a crackpot and a denizen of an irrational scientific underworld. A German, he had retired from a successful career as a merchant to devote himself to experimental farming and the writing of polemics. When the Communists took power briefly in Bavaria in 1919, the 57-year-old Gesell joined the Soviet Republic as its Finance Minister. When it collapsed, he was court-martialed, but avoided execution.

Gesell was, however, by no means a Marxist. He believed in a highly competitive economic system kept on an even keel by an ingenious type of monetary manipulation coupled with the nationalization of land.

His starting point was the discovery that throughout history the interest rate had remained comparatively constant, whereas the earning power of capital had not. He inferred that the stickiness of interest rates forced fluctuations in investment levels which caused alternating periods of boom and crisis. His proposed remedy was to impose a stamp tax on money. In order to avoid paying the tax, people would spend more rapidly, money velocities would increase, interest rates would decline and rising investment would pull the world out of depression. This program would have been beneficial during depression. The late Lord Keynes rescued Gesell's reputation from the limbo of the little groups of monetary maniacs.

It was too bad that Ezra Pound had to dabble in these matters, since he did not have the type of mind which readily grasps them. But he had now found the central, unifying theme which he believed would impart significance to his life work of poetic creation. The motif was usury, or *usuria,* as he put it. Inflexible interest rates, he thought, produced economic disaster. And who, after all, were the usurers? They were Jews.

He then combined Gesell's theories, economic anti-semitism and an adulation of Mussolini as a symbol of ORDER. The product was a nonsensical book called *Jefferson and/or Mussolini,* which mirrored the rapid disintegration of his once powerful mind: "The fascist revolution was for the preservation of certain liberties and FOR the maintenance of a certain level of culture, certain standards of living, it was NOT a refusal to come down to a level of riches or poverty, but a refusal to surrender certain immaterial prerogatives, a refusal to surrender a great slice of the cultural heritage."

## TOWARD THE ABYSS

Pound's last decade was one of swift demoralization and loss of creative power. The sensitive ear remained, but not the mind. Having become a campfollower of the armies of terror, Ezra Pound marched into the mire of nihilism.

In 1939, he returned to the United States to spread anti-semitism and laud the nation of order and discipline where all trains ran on time. Some of his literary contemporaries took the charitable view that Pound was insane; others ostracized him. He lectured bankers on economics for hours at end—at least, those who would listen. He showed no desire to learn anything himself, but clung smugly to his obsolescent view of economic Truth.

He returned to Italy disappointed. When war came, he broadcast over the fascist radio. After Pearl Harbor, there was a brief month of silence from Ezra Pound. Then, in January 1942, he resumed his radio addresses and at once crossed the borderline between disloyalty and treason.

The Italian radio announced that Ezra Pound "will not be asked to say anything whatsoever that goes against his conscience, or anything incompatible with his duties as a citizen of the U.S.A." Whatever Pound's conscience, his duties as an American citizen did not include attempting to undermine the morale of the armed forces of his country.

In addition to being an economist and one of the few sane men in a mad world, it seems that Pound was also an expert on international law. On January 29, 1942, he announced:

"The United States has been for months illegally at war through what I consider to be the criminal acts of a President whose mental condition was not, so far as I could see, all that could or should be desired. . . ." It is difficult to see how America could be "illegally at war" when Mussolini and Hitler had first declared it. The only outlaws produced by this reasoning were the Fascist and Nazi leaders. But even this simple point escaped Pound.

A few months later, he broadcast some incoherent jargon that may have been calculated to impress the men on Amercian warships: "I ask whether the spirit of '76 is helped by a-floodin' the lower ranks of the navy with bridge-sweepin's. . . ."

On May 26th, he told the American people: "Every reform, every lurch toward the just price, toward the control of a market is an act of homage to Mussolini and Hitler. They are your leaders. . . ." These four words were, in all probability, enough to entitle Pound to the electric chair had he been sane enough to stand trial for them.

His other broadcast ideas were also shoddy things clad in an incoherent vocabulary—hardly worth risking a life to express. For instance, the poet had ideas on the peace. It "will not be based on international lending. Get that for one . . . England certainly will have nothing whatever to say about what its terms are. Neither, I think, will simple-hearted Joe Stalin, not wholly trusted by the kikery, which is his master."

He wrote former American friends in less cautious terms—the broadcasts were perhaps both a mirror of cerebral decomposition and of a squirming sort of cowardice. These letters laid bare an ugly streak of sadism and insensitivity. The civil war in Spain, he told Williams, was of "no more importance than the draining of some mosquito swamp in deepest Africa." He exulted over Gestapo butcheries on the Eastern Front, referring to "fresh meat on the Russian steppes." He spoke of "Hitler the martyr."

America, Ezra Pound declared, "never had a chance in this war." In reply, when Mussolini's papier-maché war machine collapsed the American military placed Pound in a prison camp near Pisa. His new leisure time went into writing the *Pisan Cantos,* to which none of his captors bothered to object.

## THE VERDICT

Eventually, he was flown to Washington to stand trial for treason. Four alienists, after examining him and his writings, concluded:

"At the present time he exhibits extremely poor judgment as to his situation, its seriousness and the manner in which the charges are to be met. He insists that his broadcasts were not treasonable, but that all of his radio activities have stemmed from his self appointed mission to 'save the Constitution.' He is abnormally grandiose, is expansive and exuberant in manner, exhibiting pressure of speech, discursiveness, and distractibility.

"In our opinion, with advancing years his personality, for so many years abnormal, has undergone further distortion to the extent that he is now suffering from a paranoid state which renders him mentally unfit to advise properly with counsel or to participate intelligently and reasonably in his own defense. He is, in other words, insane and mentally unfit for trial, and is in need of care in a mental hospital."

On the basis of this report, a jury in the District of Columbia decided on February 13, 1946, that Ezra Pound was of "unsound mind."

## POETIC JUSTICE

Pound now sits in a comfortable room in St. Elizabeth's Hospital on the outskirts of Washington. Friends and admirers supply him with books. He is writing more verse and studying Chinese.

This last fact apparently infuriated the poet, Robert Hillyer, who composed an article for the *Saturday Review of Literature* (June 18, 1949) in which he implied that a man sane enough to learn Chinese was also sane enough for hanging. But the asylums are, as a matter of fact, sprinkled with linguists and mathematical wizards. Hillyer was on more solid ground when he objected that the comfort of the poet's surroundings "may with just indignation be contrasted to the crowded wards in which are herded the soldiers who lost their minds, defending America, which Pound hated and betrayed."

There is at least poetic justice in the conclusion to the Pound affair, which is far more instructive than the crude alternative of penitentiary or execution. If the alienists were right in their unanimous judgment, the one American representative of Western culture who betrayed democracy to the fascists was a lunatic.

Thus adjudged, Ezra Pound cannot afford to be cured. Once he steps out of St. Elizabeth's he must stand trial for treason. The alienists decided that he was too unbalanced to stand trial, but they did not conclude that he had been mad when he took traitor's pay from Mussolini's government.

The Communist publication *New Masses* issued a symposium on Ezra Pound "in which all the contributors declared he should be executed forthwith, some favoring hanging, some shooting." This was before Pound had been brought to trial and at a time when no jury had found him guilty, but Communist notions of democracy, justice and civil rights are, of course, more than slightly different from our own. In the People's Democracies, the judicial process frequently begins after officials have already returned the *Alice in Wonderland* decision, "Off with their heads!"

But even from the standpoint of political expediency, the Communists were short-sighted. Hanging an eminent American poet would have given fascism an aura of martyrdom which it did not deserve. The jury's restraint in taking nothing from Ezra Pound except his dignity and stature as a man is to be commended.


## THE BOLLINGEN AWARD

Ezra Pound's betrayal stirred a tempest in the world of American verse. The literary world was further agitated when, in early 1949, a Library of Congress committee of eminent American poets granted him the Bollingen Award for *The Pisan Cantos*—the poems he had written as a military prisoner in Italy.

When the irrelevancies were stripped off, the intellectuals' attack on Pound boiled down to the belief that the rottenness of Pound's philosophy and the anti-human role which he had played in the world struggle of the thirties had also corrupted his poetry. This is very different from saying that because a man is a traitor he cannot be a great writer. It involves judging his work in terms of its content as well as its form, insisting that the meaning of poetry is as important as its cadence.

Unfortunately, Pound's assailants were not always clear as to the importance of this distinction, although it is the very knife edge separating literary criticism in the totalitarian states from that in a democratic society.

The fact that an artist holds ideas which we believe are not only wrong but pernicious obviously does not disqualify his work. If Pound hated the Jews, Dostoevsky had similar feelings about the Germans. If Pound wanted Western science and democracy ground into the *kulturkampf* of Hitler and Mussolini, Dostoevsky held not dissimilar views about Imperial Russia vis-a-vis the West. We cannot praise Dostoevsky merely because Czarism is a distant memory and castigate Pound because the enormity of fascism is of recent date.

The issue then is the work itself. The critics are most relevant when they assert that Pound's influence over poetry has been, on the whole, degenerative; that he has helped alienate poetry from life;

that he has distorted song into acrostics for the pseudo-learned; and that, wherever he has plagiarized, he has also polluted. If all this is true—and the present writer feels incompetent to express any personal judgment—then the parallel between Pound's poetry and Pound's politics is so close that one must inevitably shed light on the other.

The Bollingen Award was a triumph for Ezra Pound, but, in a sense, also a culminating defeat. He may have been amused at the official verdict that America's greatest poetry was being written by a madman under indictment for treason. But a more significant consideration was that such an award, whether substantively right or wrong, could have been made at all. In judging Pound's poems without reference to his treason, the Bollingen committee revealed the immense vitality of the American tradition of liberalism which Pound had sought so vainly to destroy.

# Treason

> I have not found thee in the tent,
> In the broken darkness.
> I have not found thee at the well-head
> Anon, the women with pitchers . . .

When the author of these lines, Ezra Pound, came bounding out of Idaho in 1900, he brought along one of the world's remarkable egos. He also brought a poetic flame, the divining eye of a natural teacher, and a noble personality—part despot, part poet, part press agent. Clearly, he was in for a feasting time.

At 22, Pound forsook his country: the U. S. would not leave off rustling its bank notes to listen to him. The separation was final. London listened more attentively. There Pound began to publish his opaque, lapidary, brilliantly polished poems. Some of the literati began to call him the master verse maker of his generation.

*Cape, Strut, & Whiskers.* Then came Paris. The Idahoan with the glittering eye and the positive manner romped magnificently from salon to bordello, flaunting his cape and stick and Byronic collars, spitting critical fire, pinching the ladies and wagging his fierce red whiskers. He grew as famous as his neighbors, James Joyce, Gertrude Stein and Ernest Hemingway. By the time he was forty he had written 31 books. The stream of poetry, prose and French and Chinese translations swelled to a torrent. Then the early thirties, Ezra Pound stepped abruptly out of the field.

*Fascismo.* From a frouzy *pallazo* in Rapallo, Italy, he began sending out ranting political letters dated by the Fascist calendar.

---

* Courtesy *Time;* copyright Time Inc. 1945.

Friends found him extolling the "order" Mussolini had brought, prophesying wonders for Fascism and grunting over the mysteries of politics and Social Credit.

War gave Pound the international voice his poetry had failed to give him. On the Rome radio, he used it to heap contumely on the Jews, to lecture and vilify his native land. After the U. S. entered the war, he kept it up. On July 26, 1943, he became one of the few U. S. citizens ever to be indicted for treason.

Last week, the reluctant native Ezra Pound, 60, was home to stay. The positive manner was gone with the cape and the stick; his eyes were rheumy, his beard wilted. His lawyer in the capital's U. S. District Court, where he stood indicted on 19 counts of treason, said senility had made him unfit for trial, and asked that he be placed under psychiatric observation.

Police reporters sought him out as they never had before. A few scholars and fellow poets saw in his case the ancient problem of the artist *v.* society. Jurists, who anticipated the most sensational case of its kind since the trial of Aaron Burr, wondered just how the U. S. proposed to convict its disaffected poet.

*Voice of Confusion.* The ragbaggy old darling of the U. S. expatriate intelligentsia did not seem to care very much. Lolling in the infirmary of the D. C. jail, he denied that he ever talked treason: "I was only trying to tell the people of Europe and America how they could avoid war by learning the facts about money." He spoke ruefully: "It's all very well to die for an idea, but to die for an idea you can't remember. . . ." He struck a conspiratorial tone: "I took Mussolini an economic theory that could have blown the roof off Europe."

But most of the time he just sat, wrapped in his grey flannel bathrobe and his artistic and political frustrations. The tents were still empty of whoever it was he had sought.

*Newsweek,* January 7, 1946

# Impounded Records

Ezra Pound's psychiatric case records are under lock and key at St. Elizabeth's Hospital in Washington, where he is confined in a ward for the criminally insane. So many curious psychiatrists have gone there to look at the records hospital officials were afraid they might be mislaid or lost. Incidentally, some who have looked into the case believe the poet is sane enough to stand trial for treason.

# Pound's Mind "Unsound"

## Verdict Saves Writer From Standing Trial

WASHINGTON, Feb. 13 (AP)—A Federal District Court jury to-day found Ezra Pound, 60-year-old expatriate poet, to be mentally unsound. The verdict saved Pound from standing trial on treason charges arising out of his wartime writings and broadcasts in Italy.

Earlier in the day, two doctors testified that they considered the eccentric poet unfit for a treason trial.

Dr. Wendell Muncie, psychiatrist of the Johns Hopkins Hospital, said that Pound was unable to pursue a coherent line of reasoning on any subject and "is unable to give a logical statement of any phase of his case."

Dr. Marion King, medical director of the United States Public Health Service, said he considered Pound "a sensitive, eccentric, cynical person" now in "a paranoic state of psychotic proportions which renders him unfit for trial."

*Newsweek,* February 25, 1946

# Pound Foolish

At a sanity hearing in Washington last week Ezra Pound, 60-year-old poet and expatriate under indictment for treason, caused an uproar by springing to his feet and shouting, "I never did believe in Fascism. God damn it! I oppose Fascism." Quieted by his lawyer, Pound dropped his head dejectedly on the table. Four court-appointed psychiatrists who testified were unanimous: Pound was mentally unfit; he suffered from delusions of grandeur, believing it was his mission to save the United States Constitution. The court's verdict: Pound is of unsound mind; unfit to stand trial.

# Medical Report on Pound

Federal Security Agency
Saint Elizabeth's Hospital
Washington 20, D. C.

December 14, 1945

Honorable Bolitha J. Laws
Chief Justice, U. S. District Court
Washington, D. C.

Sir:

The undersigned hereby respectfully report the results of their mental examination of Ezra Pound, now detained in Gallinger Hospital by transfer for observation from the District jail on a charge of treason. Three of us (Drs. Gilbert, King, and Overholser) were appointed by your Honor to make this examination. At our suggestion, and with your approval, Dr. Wendell Muncie, acting upon the request of counsel for the accused, made an examination with us and associates himself with us in this joint report. Dr. Muncie spent several hours with the defendant, both alone and with us, on December 13, 1945, and the others of us have examined the defendant each on several occasions, separately and together, in the period from his admission to Gallinger Hospital on December 4, 1945 to December 13, 1945. We have had available to us the reports of laboratory, psychological and special physical examinations of the defendant and considerable material in the line of his writings and biographical data.

The defendant, now 60 years of age and in generally good physical condition, was a precocious student, specializing in literature. He has been a voluntary expatriate for nearly 40 years, living in England and France, and for the past 21 years in Italy, making an uncertain living by writing poetry and criticism. His poetry and literary criticism have achieved considerable recognition, but of recent years his preoccupation with monetary theories and economics has apparently obstructed his literary productivity. He has long been recognized as eccentric, querulous, and egocentric.

At the present time he exhibits extremely poor judgment as to his situation, its seriousness and the manner in which the charges are to be met. He insists that his broadcasts were not treasonable, but that all of his radio activities have stemmed from his self appointed mission to "save the Constitution." He is abnormally grandiose, is expansive and exuberant in manner, exhibiting pressure of speech, discursiveness, and distractibility.

In our opinion, with advancing years his personality, for many years abnormal, has undergone further distortion to the extent that he is now suffering from a paranoid state which renders him mentally unfit to advise properly with counsel or to participate intelligently and reasonably in his own defense. He is, in other words, insane and mentally unfit for trial, and is in need of care in a mental hospital.

Respectfully submitted,

Joseph L. Gilbert, M.D.

Wendell Muncie, M.D.

Marion R. King, M.D.

Winfred Overholser, M.D.

# A Note on the Obvious

by GEORGE DILLON*

Not all the readers of this magazine have followed it regularly through the years, and some will rightly wonder what motive any periodical may have in publishing a new work by Ezra Pound. I am as much surprised as any of our readers to see Pound re-emerging in print. If I am going to be honest, I can do as little about it.

I should have welcomed a few more months, or years, in which to get the right perspective on such an event. But there is no time schedule in this part of the world for literary production. In the United States, Pound is free to publish anything an editor will accept—including even his political balderdash, which is sometimes (but not often) entertaining and stimulating. The official medical verdict, declaring him unaccountable on psychological grounds for his collaboration with the late Italian government, is actually beside the point. This new poem is excellent. I should still publish it if the author were not in a hospital but in a cell awaiting execution.

Of course, Pound would be a more dramatic and in many eyes a more interesting figure if he had been found guilty. But let us keep the issues clear. The fact that he was so unformidable as a conspirator should not lead us to underrate him as a poet. It seems that the epilogue to his career is to be written in America, and he will, I suppose, go on publishing his work in this country. It will probably appear in book form, for the most part, because his long

---

* Mr. Dillon was editor of *Poetry* and in this article was introducing a symposium of essays on Ezra Pound.

Cantos do not easily lend themselves to magazine publication. They are a medley of five or six languages, all inaccurately written, which have to be checked and rechecked by various hands before they are in shape to print. If those who are much interested in Pound get the impression that he is not being published adequately, they should remember that the same difficulties obtain now as before the war. To put it briefly, some editors find some of the Cantos less than absorbing.

Aside from all that, is there any reason why his poetry should not be published? This leads to one of those "fundamental" questions: Can you reasonably refuse to publish a poem because of what you believe to be the pernicious effect of its ideas? The answer is that that is the wrong approach to the problem. The problem does exist: even a literary magazine must occasionally deal with it. But it can be said that ideas, however absurd, do not become pernicious in written form except through the medium of dishonest, and therefore bad, writing. (Which is not to say that honest writing cannot also be bad.) If we are thinking of our hard-defended rudiments of democracy, I can imagine no danger to them from one who writes as candidly as Pound does. His political ideas, appearing as what they are, have only their proper effect, which is peevish and trivial. He could never compare as a menace with some of the uncandid engineers of opinion and their hired scribes, whether in business or journalism or government—those highly respected and patriotic big operators who supported fascism up to the moment war was declared.

I confess that it is hard for me, in my own mind, to disentangle Pound from the war. His voice is associated with a certain shack in the mid-African heat, and even more with a narrow, brilliantly lighted radio tunnel under Plymouth harbor. There, in the invasion period, when we dialed the short-wave programs during rest intervals, Pound was sometimes good for five minutes of modest entertainment. That is all it was, and I doubt whether any of us who listened to him felt anything but amusement, though we were not in a kindly mood. Often the stuttering signal from France would go dead when a station was threatened or hit. Pound, whenever we caught his performance, went on and on. But it was impossible to have any serious reaction. One night, feeling out of sorts and turning him off in mild abhorrence, I ran directly on to one of those broad-casts of underground code phrases that sounded like surrealist poetry, and heard the words solemnly declaimed in French: "Re-serve an amiable reception for the acrobat," which I have since associated with Pound. At the moment it seemed to suggest the right spirit in which to listen to him. It still does.

Because the verdict, anti-climax that it is, is right. I cannot help reflecting that many of those who were walking about Plymouth Hoe at that time have not come back, and that Pound is among us, though he may not wish to be, and beginning to publish his writing. But I realize that this is a chance irony: there is no connection between the two facts. In this new autobiographical poem, speaking with nostalgia of England and France, he uses the word "contrition" —make of it what you will—and asks for "oblivion not forgive-ness." I have not been told how he feels about being here. The fact remains that an important, though frequently mad, writer has returned to his country (he would be an important writer if it were only for his influence on Eliot and Yeats), to begin what is necessarily a new period. *Poetry* signalizes that fact with the following essays, which I think remarkably fine, reviewing his career and analyzing his art.

On the other hand, there is no reason why we should be happier than one may suppose Pound to be about his repatriation. He has always seemed the expatriate *sub specie aeternitatis*. It is interesting, however, to hear those rejoice who are minded to do so—hailing him, in R. P. Blackmur's figure, as a bright star persisting in an un-welcome dawn.

I thought it was about time for someone to begin quoting the lines from *Mauberley*. They were very plausible twenty years ago, in reaction from a great deal of cant. And now? The dreadful image has become almost companionable. Perhaps just because so many have died for her, the "old bitch gone in the teeth" should be allowed her points. Anyone who went to Germany after 1930 must know that we were up against something very much rottener in the last war, though with a full set of teeth. It is not necessary to have seen, or heard about, such places as Buchenwald. In Italy the rottenness was less obvious for those practiced in looking the other way.

But the contributors speak for themselves. If the other editors and I can truthfully say that we are happy to publish this poem, it is because there could be no better proof that we are able to publish what we please. Our satisfaction is in the thoughtful exercise of that freedom, and not, of course, in demonstrating it to Pound: its meaning happens to be one he mysteriously doesn't get. Yet its meaning is the sum total of all those one-way tickets across the Channel. The ivory towers, however costly and useless, are paid for.

# Reviews of *Cantos* and *The Pisan Cantos*

Pound, Ezra Loomis. *Cantos* (538p) $5 New Directions.

"For more than twenty years Ezra Pound has been at work on a monumental poem of epic scale—The Cantos. . . . The present volume brings together all the Cantos which have been completed to date. 'A Draft of XXX Cantos,' 'Eleven New Cantos,' 'The Fifth Decad of Cantos,' and 'Cantos LII-LXXI' are reprinted here, and to them are added 'The Pisan Cantos.' "–Publisher's note

"The moral universe of the Divine Comedy was orthodox, graded, and public, firmly conceived to its uttermost corner; and this of Pound's is quite another thing. But at their least valuation I submit that these cantos in which light and air—and song—move so freely are more exhilarating poetic sketch books, 'Notes from the Upper Air,' than can be found elsewhere in our literature." Robert Fitzgerald New Republic 119:31 Ag 16 '48 1750w

"Pound's sense of language is inferior to none, in spite of his large abuse of it. He is sometimes betrayed by a desire to make English do the work of the Chinese ideographs with which the text is peppered, and there are large dull stretches in which he rambles on, mulling over memories of men and books, trivial anecdotes, old animosities, talking unintelligibly to himself. But the last passages in the Cantos, which move between verse as speech and

* This selection is reprinted in full, including references to further reviews, from the *Book Review Digest.*

verse as song, are, in either genre, supreme." *New York Herald Tribune* wkly Bk R. p. 7 Ag 22 '48 550 w

"The whole design is gradually becoming plain. Pound's apparent intention is to present 'ideas in action'; the living ideas of the past to counteract the dead ideas of the modern world, in which usury has triumphed." Lloyd Frankenberg NY Times p 14 Ag 1 '48 350w

Reviewed by Louise Bogan *New Yorker* 24:107 O 30 '48 480w
Reviewed by W. V. O'Connor *Sat R* 31:15 S 4 '48 400w
                              *Time* 52:110 O 25 850w
Reviewed by L. L. Martz *Yale R* n s 39:144 Autumn '48 1100w

Pound, Ezra Loomis. *Pisan Cantos* 118p $2.75 New Directions

"These ten Cantos, called 'The Pisan Cantos' because they were composed when the poet was incarcerated in a prison camp near Pisa, are the most recent additions to the monumental epic poem on which Pound has been working for more than twenty years. . . . Writing entirely out of memory . . . they are more autobiographical than many of the earlier sections." Publisher's note

Reviewed by Leo Kennedy *Chicago Sun* Ag 9 '48 650w
Reviewed by Rolfe Humphries *Nation* 167:349 S 25 '48 650w
Reviewed by Robert Fitzgerald *New Report* 119:21
                              Ag 16 '48 1750 w
Reviewed by Babette Deutsch
                *N Y Herald Tribune Wkly* Bk R p7 Ag 22 '48 550 w
Reviewed by Lloyd Frankenberg *N Y Times* p14 Ag 1 '48 350w

"Pound's imprisonment in Pisa seems to have brought him back to art and to life. 'The Pisan Cantos' shows a new sense of proportion. He begins to feel pity and gratitude, and he begins to smile wryly, even at himself. I cannot think of any other record by an artist or a man of letters, in or out of prison, so filled with a combination of sharp day-to-day observation, erudition, and humorous insight." Louise Bogan *New Yorker* 24:107 O 30 '48 480w

Reviewed by Reed Whittemore, *Poetry* 73:108 N '48 900w
Reviewed by T. H. Ferril, *San Francisco Chronicle*
p11 N 7 '48 160w
Reviewed by W. V. O'Connor, *Sat R of Lit* 31:15 S 4 '48 400w
Reviewed by L. L. Martz, *Yale R* n s 38:144 *autumn* '48 1100w

A letter in *Esquire,* February, 1958\*

# The Cage

by ROBERT L. ALLEN

We saw flakes of blue light coming from the stockade at the Dis. ciplinary Training Center one night in May of 1945. Acetylene torches, someone said; later we heard that they were reinforcing a cage to hold Ezra Pound.

The Disciplinary Training Center spread over a broad field a few miles north of Pisa on the road to Viareggio. The ugly barbed-wire stockade held back the slime and filth of the whole Mediterranean Theater of Operations: convicted rapists, murderers, and traitors who had been members of our Armed Forces. Each "trainee" was on his way to a federal prison in the United States—unless he could "soldier out" of the DTC.

By following a fantastic routine, accepting cruelty in the extreme, and by turning himself into a "G.I." automaton, a trainee could have his federal prison term canceled and be returned to duty. This took a lot of guts or a lot of hate and not all men could do it. Some of them tried to run away one afternoon, but businesslike short bursts from an automatic rifle in a guard tower chopped them down. (I rode to the hospital with two of them while they bled to death.) Some had a try at suicide and others poured lye on their feet to earn a trip to the hospital in Pisa.

Inside the stockade there was a secondary enclosure for the Medical and Dental sections, two mess halls, several areas where the trainees pitched their pup tents, and solitary confinement and death

\* Reprinted from *Esquire,* February 1958 © 1958 by Esquire, Inc.

cells. The solitary cells, "boxes," were seven-foot concrete cubes with peepholes in their steel doors. To be "boxed" meant two weeks on bread and water with a blanket and a bucket. The death cells were wire cages about ten feet square at the base and seven feet high. Condemned prisoners, later to be hanged at Aversa, paced the cages.

The jailers at the DTC (the Headquarters Company, Provost, Guard, and Medical sections) lived in pyramidal tents outside the stockade. We had our own mess hall, recreation hall and stables (the colonel liked to ride). The Provost Section men had the most to do with the prisoners. Their whim was law to the trainees and their job was to assure that life as a trainee was tougher than life at the front. It was interesting to observe how quickly many of the new men in the Provost Section learned to enjoy their work. The Provost boys were in charge of Ezra Pound.

The morning after we had seen the acetylene torches, all DTC personnel were ordered to keep clear of Pound; no one was to speak to him. I recognized him easily by the beard and the glasses. His molting, amber Vandyke was not the red beard that once bounded through the salons and cafés of London and Paris. The Ezra Pound in the cage was a frustrated old man who had never received the recognition he desired—recognition that came to a number of his associates.

He wore an Army fatigue uniform, unbuttoned at the neck. He walked back and forth on the concrete floor, making no effort to look outside. His trousers hung loose and his shoes were unlaced. (Belts and shoelaces were always taken from men in the cages.) A special guard stood outside his cage which, at night, was brightly lighted. Everyone looked at him. The trainees marching by or working in the area considered Pound with awe, taking the reinforced cage as evidence that he was a particularly tough customer.


### LIFE IN A CAGE

The United States authorities had taken him into custody at Rapallo where he made his home, and brought him directly to the DTC. The weeks in the cage were hard on Pound. As shelter, a piece of tar paper was thrown over the top. Also he had a pup tent which, quite ingeniously, he pitched in several different ways. Later he told me of spending hours watching wasps construct a nest and of his fascination with the work of an ant colony. He was permitted books and writing materials, but refused a typewriter because, he said, the "damned dust would ruin it." His daily exercises caused quite a stir. He would engage in imaginary tennis matches, making graceful, looping forehands and backhands. He assumed fencing stances and danced nimbly about the cage, shadow boxing.

"What's he training for?" one of the trainees asked me.

Through his antics, he became a camp character and after a while he exchanged a few clandestine words each day with the trainees who brought his food. Because the dust and harsh sun in the cage inflamed his eyes, he was transferred to a tent within the Medical Compound. His furniture was an Army cot and a small wooden packing crate; later a second packing crate and a table were added.

During the first week or so in the Medical Compound he kept to himself in his tent. His food, eaten from an Army mess kit, was handed to him through the Medical Compound fence. He soon stripped off his Army fatigue clothes and spent the warm summer days comfortably attired only in Army olive drab underwear, a fatigue cap, G.I. shoes and socks.

He found an old broom handle that became a tennis racquet, a billiard cue, a rapier, a baseball bat to hit small stones and a stick which he swung out smartly to match his long stride. His constitutionals wore a circular path in the compound grass.


## HE TALKED FREELY

It was arranged for Pound to come on sick call after the trainees and to receive treatment, if necessary, in the evenings. Foot baths and eye drops were the most frequent prescriptions on his card. Far from being reticent in talking about his case, he seemed anxious to discuss the charges against him and we in the Medical Section were a good audience. He claimed that he would never be brought to trial because he "had too much on several people in Washington" for the Government to allow him to testify in court. He admitted that he had made broadcasts from Rome, but said that they were in no way treasonable and that he had never supported the Fascists. His connection with Mussolini was brushed off lightly with a laugh. He said that he had seen "Muss" (or "Ben") once and then they had talked only for a short time about nonpolitical matters. It was clear that Mussolini had not given him the time or attention he thought his economic theories warranted. After his evening treatment, he would stride to the door of our prefab, put his crumpled Army fatigue hat onto the back of his head, tuck his stick under his arm and wave an appreciative and smiling good night.

Pound's conduct was a welcome topic of conversation at the DTC. His sanity was questioned not only by trainees but also, eventually, by the camp psychiatrist. Stories about Pound's interview with the psychiatrist flew around the camp—a trainee working with the psychiatrist had told a friend about it. Pound, always spoken of as "Ezra," became sort of a hero among the trainees when word was spread that he had "made a dummy of the psychiatrist"—that he had turned questions around so that even the psychiatrist became confused. In the end, the unofficial opinion of the psychiatrist was that Ezra Pound was sane, although perhaps "a little exotic," as one of my friends put it.

Throughout the summer of 1945 Pound was in excellent spirits. He was granted permission to use the dispensary typewriter in the evening and it was not unusual to see him typing a letter to some trainee's girl or mother with the trainee dictating at his shoulder and Pound interpreting for him.


## WORKED AT NIGHT

After taps when all trainees were in their tents, Pound worked on his *Cantos* and Chinese translations. The constant clanging and banging of the typewriter, which he punched angrily with his index fingers, were always accompanied by a high-pitched humming sound he made as the carriage raced the bell. He swore well and profusely over typing errors.

During the late evenings the only person with him was the Charge of Quarters and often, after typing, Pound would let down completely to rant and rave about the "dunghill usurers" and "usuring cutthroats." Among others, he damned Mussolini ("the crude peasant"), Hitler, FDR, Churchill, and Henry Morgenthau. His green eyes snapped as he tapped his glasses on the desk and shouted that the American people had been swindled on monetary exchanges. He insisted that wars could be avoided if the true nature of money were understood. "When," he would ask, "will the United States return to Constitutional government?"

The rainy, grey fall weather came and Pound's tent was anything but comfortable. His request for more blankets was delayed for a week while an officious corporal pondered the matter.

## BOOKS BECAME HIS LIFE

He became extremely depressed. One evening I borrowed a book of Chinese translations from him. "Please, don't lose it and return it in the morning," he said. "It's my very blood and bone." He told us that when he was picked up in May, he had expected to be flown directly to Washington. Even when the vehicle carrying him stopped at the DTC, he thought that his visit would end as soon as a plane was readied at Pisa airfield. Then, in that cold, wet fall, with no indication of when the occupation of Italy would be terminated, he almost despaired of ever leaving Pisa.

He read voraciously—novels, magazines, everything that was given to him. The Mediterranean edition of *The Stars and Stripes* and the overseas editions of *Time* and *Newsweek* were his sources of news. Early in November *The Stars and Stripes* carried a story that six Italian radio technicians were to be flown to Washington to testify at a grand-jury investigation of his case. Pound knew that, in order to establish him as a traitor, the Justice Department would have to produce at least two witnesses who had seen him commit a treasonous act. At first he made light of the whole story and asserted that no one had ever seen him broadcast. He said that the six technicians were obviously impostors "just making the flight to get some decent food."

His last two weeks at the DTC were the most difficult for him. His tone of conversation changed and occasionally he spoke of him-

self in the past tense. Several times he said, "If I go down, someone must carry on."

One evening after taps in the middle of November, Pound was
sitting in the dispensary reading Joseph E. Davies' *Mission to Mos-
cow*. The Charge of Quarters sat at the desk next to him. From
time to time Pound commented on the book. Suddenly the door
opened and two young lieutenants entered. They told Pound that
he would be flown to Washington in one hour and to get his personal effects together. They turned and left. Pound handed the book
to the C.Q. He asked him to thank all of the medical personnel for
their kindness. He then walked to the door of the prefab, turned
and, with a half-smile, put both hands around his neck to form a
noose and jerked up his chin.

Hanover, N.H.

*Poetry,* January, 1949

# The Background of *The Pisan Cantos*

by DAVID PARK WILLIAMS

The recently published *Pisan Cantos* of Ezra Pound contain numerous references to persons and locales connected with the stockade where Pound was imprisoned. My experience as a guard at the Disciplinary Training Center near Pisa (the "D.T.C." in Canto LXXVI, p. 33) when Pound was there from May through October, 1945, gives me a certain familiarity with the background of which he speaks. It seems to me that a few notes on the D.T.C. personalities and local color referred to by Pound might heighten a reader's appreciation of the new *Cantos.*

For example, the remark of the "cheerful reflective nigger" in Canto LXXVIII, page 57, "Steele that is one awful name," conveys nothing unless one knows that Lt. Col. Steele was the stockade commander, an office with unpleasant associations for prisoners. The names of the speaker's companions, Blood and Slaughter, are not allegorical, but were actually the cognomens of two prisoners I knew. The Colonel's position made "Steele" a far more "awful" surname than either "Slaughter" or "Blood."

Pound speaks often of the "death cells," meaning half a dozen cages and sixty "boxes" where so-called "incorrigibles" were locked up. Actually, the term "death cells" is a misnomer, for capital punishment was not usual at the D.T.C. The cages, which held escape-artists and especially dangerous criminals such as members of the Lane gang (Canto LXXIV, p. 6), were constructed of a heavy wire, enabling the guards to keep a twenty-four hour watch on those within. The first of these cages was torn down when Pound was brought to the D.T.C., and a new enclosure of heavy grillwork was built in its place. This was the "gorilla cage" (Canto LXXXIII, page 111) in which Ezra Pound was incarcerated for several weeks. The authorities took the precaution of constructing a stronger cell because of an alleged fear that Italian fascists would attempt to rescue the accused traitor. No such attempt at rescue was ever made. Pound slept on the cement floor of his cage (Canto LXXVII, p. 48), with only a tar paper roof above him by day; at night he was permitted to rig a pup tent inside the cage to keep out the cold. The closing couplet of the *Cantos* is particularly apt:

"If the hoar frost grip thy tent
Thou wilt give thanks when night is spent."

Behind the cages stood the "boxes," concrete cells just large enough for a man to stand up or lie down. Solitary confinement there meant two weeks on bread and water. Whiteside, the Negro turnkey (Canto LXXIV, p. 14, and Canto LXXIX, p. 63), opened the iron doors of the cells once a day to distribute the meager rations. Stocky and grave, a person beautiful in his simplicity, he was the bearer of news and refreshment to Pound and the other caged men. No wonder the poet calls Whiteside "God's messenger."

Pound's volume of Confucius (Canto LXXX, p. 76) was by his side continually, and the prisoner read for hours, or simply sat and combed his ragged beard, watching the Pisa road where passers-by and an occasional white ox were visible (Canto LXXIV, p. 6). Pound speaks of lying "with Barabbas and 2 thieves," an analogy more notable for its drama than for its humility. The poet had ample time to listen to the conversations of both criminals and guards, and his quotations are remarkably well chosen, reflecting the general attitude of men in the Pisa stockade. The guard's statement on page 14 is thoroughly typical of a sentiment one heard over and over again at the D.T.C. (Anyone familiar with armed forces vocabulary can translate the abbreviations in this passage, or in the one opposite.) The reference, on the same page, to "a bag o' Dukes" concerns the prison custom of using cigarettes or "roll-your-own" tobacco as the unit of exchange in all commercial transactions. Money was strictly forbidden, and tobacco was rationed according to a man's company status. A new arrival was placed in what was known as a "second-class company," where he received a small ration of "Dukes Mixture" or "Bull Durham" weekly. Three or four months of good behavior brought promotion to a "first-class company," where the ration was increased. Failure to make good marks in inspection brought demotion to third class, where there was no tobacco ration at all.

The prisoners were known officially as "trainees," a term often coupled with the adjective "god-damned" (as in Canto LXXX, p. 76), although, as Pound points out, they were really "man-damned." Pound appears fascinated by the number of trainees who bore the names of ex-presidents of the United States; I remember a Washington, very dark and distinguished-looking, and also poor Tyler, who escaped through the window of a hospital prison ward, only to be brought back to the stockade next day in his pajamas and bathrobe.

The barbed-wire-enclosed area surrounding the "death cells" was one of many separate compounds inside the stockade fence— Pound's "10,000 gibbet-iform posts supporting barbed wire" (Canto LXXVII, p. 51). The "gibbet" arms of the posts supported charged wires, probably those wires on which Pound saw birds sitting like musical notes (Canto LXXXII, p. 103, and elsewhere).

The "4 giants in 4 corners" (pages 7, 8, and 43) may easily refer to the fact that of the fourteen "guard roosts" (Canto LXXIV, p. 6), only the four at the corners of the stockade were equipped with Browning Automatic Rifles (B-A-Rs). Guards in the other ten towers carried Thompson sub-machine guns, which were far inferior to the B-A-Rs in accuracy and distance. This gave the guards in the corner posts the comparative stature of "giants." Eight men from the Special Company (a unit made up of mental cases) were mowed down by the B-A-Rs while attempting to escape across the drill field. The break occurred during Pound's stay at the D.T.C., and the Special Company area was located only a few yards from Pound's cage. This may explain the poet's absorption with the corner towers.

The sounds of the D.T.C. play an important part in *The Pisan Cantos*. Troops were often punished with close-order drill after dark in what was known as "Number Ten Area" of the stockade; the peculiar sing-song commands of the Negro trainee non-coms seem hinted in Canto LXXX, page 76. In addition to the extra "moon-light drill," the trainees underwent fourteen hours of training daily. The monotonous beat of the "bumm drum" in the prison band is mentioned on pages 6, 63, and 65. Pound heard it often.

Exercises included obstacle running (pp. 12, 51), and parading with real rifles (the firing-pins removed). The "banners" (Canto LXXIV, p. 6—actually guidons) were red for first-class companies and blue for second-class. Guards on foot and on horseback pa-trolled the circuit of the drill field when the troops were out ("the young horse whinnies against the tubas"—Canto LXXIX, p. 63). The mention of band, flag, and staff car on pages 63, 64, and 65 suggests a Saturday full-field inspection, for it was then that trainees who had won Clemency and freedom were released from the stock-ade as honorable soldiers on probation. Fourteen months was the average stay of a trainee under the Clemency system; the length of his sentence didn't matter if his record was good. Work on the "honey wagon" (Canto LXXX, p. 76), which collected excrement from the stockade latrines, was a speedy and popular way of earn-ing good marks and Clemency.

"The ripper" (pp. 35, 77) was a provost sergeant who may well have administered many of the supposedly secret clubbings of re-calcitrant prisoners. His nickname, however, was derived from his habit of ripping all unfastened buttons from a trainee's uniform; a missing button could delay a man's Clemency for months.

Pound did not remain longer than a few weeks in his "gorilla cage," probably because of his increasingly poor health. He was moved from the cage to the medical area, where he spent most of the summer and part of the fall of 1945 in his own pyramidal tent. (Hence the "smoke-hole" episodes in Cantos LXXVI and LXXVII.) Pound's pyramidal was pitched near the hospital tents which sheltered trainees "on quarters." Also nearby was the latrine Pound mentions as the place where he heard the war was over (Canto LXXVII, pp. 44 and 45). Apparently, the *Cantos* were written while Pound was living in the medical area. He makes fre-quent mention of details connected with the dispensary, and quotes names from sick-call lists he heard read each day outside his tent (pp. 67, 91, 115, and elsewhere). Sick-call was about evenly divided between those who feigned illness to escape their rigorous training, and those who had concealed serious maladies for weeks so as not to spoil their chances for swift Clemency.

Pound was relatively comfortable at this time, with a cot, books, writing paper, and a packing-case "table." The gift of this table by a prisoner is surprising, yet similar incidents happened all the time. The giver's warning, "Doan you tell no one I made you that table," (pp. 12 and 63) was an eminently reasonable request from a man who might lose a meal, or even his opportunity for Clemency and freedom, if he should be caught giving aid and comfort to the accused traitor. Merely conversing with Pound was strictly *verboten,* but many trainees and guards were willing to take risks in order to remain compassionate human beings. As Pound observes (Canto LXXIV, p. 12), "the greatest . . . charity" is "to be found among those who have not observed regulations."

Library of Congress Press
Release No. 542, February 20, 1949.

# *The Pisan Cantos* Wins for Ezra Pound First Award of Bollingen in Poetry

The first annual award of the Bollingen Prize in Poetry has been made to Ezra Pound for his book the *Pisan Cantos,* it was announced today at the Library of Congress.

The Bollingen Prize in Poetry, established a year ago, was made possible by a gift of money from the Bollingen Foundation, and is to be awarded annually on the basis of a recommendation by a jury of selection consisting of the Fellows in American Letters of the Library of Congress. This is an honorary and advisory group appointed by the Librarian of Congress and consists of the following well-known writers: Conrad Aiken, W. H. Auden, Louise Bogan, Katherine Garrison Chapin, T. S. Eliot, Paul Green, Robert Lowell, Katherine Anne Porter, Karl Shapiro, Allen Tate, Willard Thorp and Robert Penn Warren, as well as Léonie Adams, the Library's Consultant in Poetry in English for the present year. Theodore Spencer (deceased January 18, 1949) was a member of the group at the time that the selection was made for the 1948 award of the Bollingen Prize; Archibald MacLeish and William Carlos Williams have become members since the selection was made.

The prize is awarded to the author of the book of verse which, in the opinion of the jury of selection, represents the highest achievement of American poetry in the year for which the award is made. The jury may, however, decline to make a selection for any given year if in its judgment no poetry worthy of the prize was published during that year. The amount of the prize is one thousand dollars.

In recommending that the award be made to Mr. Pound the jury has stated that:

> "The fellows are aware that objections may be made to awarding a prize to a man situated as is Mr. Pound. In their view, however, the possibility of such objection did not alter the responsibility assumed by the Jury of Selection. This was to make a choice for the award among the eligible books, provided any one merited such recognition, according to the stated terms of the Bollingen Prize. To permit other considerations than that of poetic achievement to sway the decision would destroy the significance of the award and would in principle deny the validity of that objective perception of value on which civilized society must rest."

# Homage to Twelve Judges (an editorial)

by DWIGHT MACDONALD

"The Fellows are aware that objections may be made to awarding a prize to a man situated as is Mr. Pound. In their view, however, the possibility of such objection did not alter the responsibility assumed by the jury of selection. . . . To permit other considerations than that of poetic achievement to sway the decision would destroy the significance of the award and would in principle deny the validity of that objective perception of value on which any civilized society must rest."

This seems to me the best political statement made in this country for some time, just as the action of the Fellows in awarding the 1948 Bollingen Prize to Ezra Pound's *The Pisan Cantos* is the brightest political act in a dark period. Let me explain why, despite the disclaimers of the Fellows themselves, I consider their award a political, as well as a literary, event.

As is well known, Mr. Pound's situation is disreputable and hopeless to a dramatic degree. For many years, he has articulated fascistic and anti-Semitic sentiments; during the war, he made radio propaganda from Italy for Mussolini's regime and against his native country; he is now under arrest in a Washington mental hospital and will be tried for treason when and if he is pronounced mentally competent. The very book for which he is now honored was mostly written in a US Army prison in Pisa, nor is it by any means free of its author's detestable social and racial prejudices.

The prize committee is a distinguished one. Its members are: Conrad Aiken, W. H. Auden, Louise Bogan, T. S. Eliot, Paul Green, Robert Lowell, Katherine Anne Porter, Karl Shapiro, the

---

* Reprinted in *Memoirs of a Revolutionist,* Meridian Books, Inc., 1958.

late Theodore Spencer, Allen Tate, Willard Thorp, and Robert Penn Warren. These constitute the Fellows in American Literature, a board appointed by Luther Evans, the Librarian of Congress. Thus we have a committee composed of eminent American writers and appointed by a high Government Official, giving an important literary prize to a man under arrest for treason. I think there are not many other countries today, and certainly none East of the Elbe where this could happen, and I think we can take some pride as Americans in having as yet preserved a society free and "open" enough for it to happen.

Whether *The Pisan Cantos* is the best poetry published by an American last year or not, I am incompetent to judge. Nor is this the point considered here, which is rather that by some miracle the Bollingen judges were able to consider Mr. Pound the poet apart from Mr. Pound the fascist, Mr. Pound the anti-Semite, Mr. Pound the traitor, Mr. Pound the funny-money crank, and all the other Mr. Pounds whose existence has properly nothing to do with the question of whether Mr. Pound the poet had or had not written the best American poetry of 1948.

"That objective perception of value on which any civilized society must rest"—this seems to me a formulation difficult to improve. Is not one of the most repellent aspects of the present Soviet system—or, for that matter, of the fascist system which Mr. Pound was so foolish as to admire—precisely that any "objective perception of value" is impossible under it? For such a perception is possible only under two closely related conditions. The first is that no one sphere of human activity is exalted over the rest. The second is that clear distinctions be maintained between the various spheres, so that the value of an artist's work or a scientist's researches is not confused with the value of their politics.

The horror of Soviet communism, of course, is that it reduces the individual to one aspect, the political. The consequence is the obliteration of the boundary lines between the various aspects of culture—or better, the imperialist conquest of all the rest by politics—so that the fifteen members of the Politburo decide, *ex cathedra,* literally all questions, including the most abstruse problems of esthetics and science. Is not the literal meaning of "totalitarianism" just this pretension of the political power to control the *totality* of human life?

Such imperfect democracy as we of the West still possess depends on our continuing ability to make the kind of discrimination the Bollingen committee made, to evaluate each sphere of human activity separate from the rest instead of enslaving them all to one great reductive tyrant, whether it be The Church, The Proletariat, People's Democracy, The Master Race or American Patriotism. Such limping justice as our courts produce likewise rests on their ability to distinguish the defendant's total behavior and personality from the specific action he is accused of having committed. And such cultural achievement as we are still capable of is nourished by "that objective perception of value on which any civilized society must rest."

The wave of the future is rolling in the other direction, as the warmaking centralized State becomes more powerful. It is ironical that it is precisely those who are misnamed "liberals" and even "socialists" who seem to be least enthusiastic about the Pound award. What bothers them is the very thing that is healthiest, politically, about it: the fact that Pound's treason and fascism were not taken into account in honoring him as a poet.

An extreme reaction was that of Albert Deutsch (whose liberalism has a Stalinoid tinge) writing in the liberal N.Y. *Post* of February 28. After a virulent column, in which he denounces Lowell and Eliot as "friends of the turncoat poet" and criticizes them because they have not turned *their* coats ("they have been faithful visitors to Pound's ward in St. Elizabeth's"), Deutsch concludes: "There is something unholy in the act. To bestow honor in any form on the man who broadcast Fascist propaganda under the auspices of the Fascist enemy of his native land smacks, to me, like Benedict Arnold's American contemporaries awarding him a medal for his undoubted military ability—after his betrayal of West Point. . . . Regardless of the protestations of the prize committee, the prize given to the turncoat poet is likely to be regarded not only as a literary event but as a political act in many parts of our world."

On which: (1) such a medal to Benedict Arnold would have been, in my opinion, a noble gesture; (2) the award is indeed, as argued above, a "political act"—and one which should demonstrate to "many parts of our world" that at least some Americans have a right to oppose Soviet totalitarianism in the name of freedom.

# A Prize for Ezra Pound

by WILLIAM BARRETT

The awarding of a prize is a public act usually surrounded with many difficulties. When the prize is literary, there are not only all the difficulties that attend literary judgment, but the further complications from the fact that the judges, because of the public nature of the award, act both as citizens and literary critics.

The Bollingen Foundation has recently announced that the Bollingen Prize for Poetry, the first of an annual series, has been awarded to Ezra Pound for *The Pisan Cantos* as the best book of poetry published during 1948. The judges were the Fellows in American Letters of the Library of Congress, among whom are T. S. Eliot, W. H. Auden, Allen Tate, Robert Penn Warren, Katherine Anne Porter, and Robert Lowell. In the public statement accompanying the award the judges tell us that they were aware that the choice of Pound was likely to provoke objections, and their brief statement implies that they have given these objections careful consideration, ending with something like an affirmation of a general principle:

> To permit other considerations than that of poetic achievement to sway the decision would destroy the significance of the award and would in principle deny the validity of that objective perception of value on which any civilized society must rest.

The sentiments behind this declaration seem to us admirable. Our only interest here is to insist on the application of this principle.

Civilization is a difficult task for all of us, requiring that we live in many different domains of human life at once, in each of which we are called on to affirm the principle of the "objective perception of value." It would be a pity if in the enthusiasm of affirming an "objective perception of value" in one direction we ceased to affirm it in another; if in the aesthetic recognition of Pound's poetry as valuable we chose to forget all about the humanly ugly attitudes of which he has been a spokesman both in his writing and in his brief and lamentable career as a broadcaster.

In this number of *Partisan Review* we print a long essay on Pound's poetry by John Berryman. Our printing of this essay is an affirmation of our belief that independent aesthetic judgment must be the continuing task of criticism, and in this belief we are clearly in agreement with the attitude enunciated by the Bollingen judges. It is not likely that Mr. Berryman has said the last word in the criticism of Pound (in these matters there is never a last word), but it is likely that he has made out the strongest possible case for Pound's having a subject matter as a poet. Mr. Berryman deals chiefly with the earlier and middle phases of Pound's career, and does not touch upon what Pound's subject matter became in recent years. This is perhaps incomplete, since our understanding of the whole career of a writer must surely take into view what his subject matter was capable of degenerating into under the pressures of personal and social disintegration. But whatever the critical truth here may be, it seems to us that Mr. Berryman's essay is in a different boat from the statement by the Bollingen judges, who were making a public award and were therefore more directly involved in public responsibilities.

Two things have to be, and are here distinguished: the case of Pound the man, and the value of the particular book, *The Pisan Cantos*. Pound the man has passed beyond the court of literary criticism into the jurisdiction of psychiatry and public justice, and it would be gratuitously vindictive for anyone to heap new tribulation on his wretched figure. Therefore our concern is, like that of the Bollingen judges, directly with the single book.

The statement by the judges shows an admirable frankness, but it is a pity that having gone so far in being frank, they did not go all the way, and actually name and face the specific objections they foresaw. The possible statement, which they might have made and the details of which each judge may have traced mentally, might then run something like this (considerations of style omitted):

"We are aware of the objections that may be raised concerning Pound's career as a fascist and anti-semite. However, under the terms of this award, we have confined our judgment to his poetry, and specifically the poetry found in the particular book under consideration, *The Pisan Cantos*. Of course, we have not missed the fact that this book itself expresses some of those unfortunate attitudes that led to Pound's downfall:

> Pétain defended Verdun while Blum
> was defending a bidet.

These lines express a vicious anti-semitic lie that was a part of the official Vichy propaganda during the War. Nevertheless, under the terms of the award, our judgment is of the poetry as poetry, and therefore we cannot reject it because of political considerations.

"To be sure, we know that the matter of these lines is not a political belief (with which we might disagree), but a deep human attitude, an emotion of hatred that is hideous, ugly and vicious and is expressed even more painfully in other lines in the book:

> the yidd is a stimulant, and the goyim are cattle
> in gt/proportion and go to saleable slaughter
> with the maximum of docility

and again:

> and the goyim are undoubtedly in great numbers cattle
> whereas a jew will receive information.

But if the reader considers these verses carefully for their rhythm and diction, their effective use of a living colloquial language, he will be led to overlook, we think, the vicious and ugly emotion expressed.

"Our problem would be much easier if this were a dramatic poem, in which this odious human attitude was expressed by one of the characters with whom the author need not be in agreement. But *The Pisan Cantos* is a lyrical poem, or group of lyrical poems, in which Pound is expressing Pound, and this ugly human attitude expressed in the lines above is one that the poet seeks to convey as his own to the reader. This has been another difficulty we have had to surmount in making our award.

"Nor do we feel that the difficulty is overcome by saying, in excuse of Pound, that this hideous attitude is the expression of a pathological mind. We know that, however privately pathological this mind may be, the attitudes it expresses are historically connected with certain objective facts like six million Jews dead in Europe, in crematory ovens or battles of extermination; and historical facts like these make it immensely more difficult to perform that necessary aesthetic judgment that separates matter from form in a poem.

"All these difficulties might have been shirked if we had chosen not to make the award at all for the year 1948. Nobody compelled us to grant this prize. Under the terms of the award, the prize need not be given in a year when no book is deemed to meet critical standards. But it seemed to us more important that all the foregoing difficulties be met, and that in the interests of civilization the aesthetic principle be affirmed that a poet's technical accomplishments can transform material that is ugly and vicious into beautiful poetry."

Naturally, it would be foolish to expect any jury of selection ever to make a statement like this. Nobody is compelled to wear his complete honesty in public; it would be tedious to assemble such a costume, and tedious to have to observe it. The brief statement accompanying the award seems to show that the judges may have traversed these details involved in their choice. We hope that they did. We hope even more that all those persons interested in literature and "civilized society" who have read the news of the award and its accompanying statement will be moved to follow through the details of the judges' difficulties outlined above.

Every particular literary judgment brings us in the end to some question of principle, and we should not like to leave the Pound case without bringing out this general question to which it has led us. During the 'thirties literature was subjected uncritically to all kinds of aesthetically distorting or irrelevant political attitudes. These political attitudes have by this time collapsed, leaving behind them a deposit of vague sentimentalities which, while obstructing any current of new political thought, still makes it impossible for many people to separate aesthetic from other considerations. When a historical movement collapses, it seems, it does not leave even the virtues of its vices. The statement by the Bollingen judges shows a laudable intention to reaffirm the validity of aesthetic principles. Our history, however, would be incomplete if we did not notice that within American literary criticism over the past decade or more there has developed another attitude which is so obsessed with formal and technical questions that it has time for only a hasty glimpse at content. Given these two conflicting tendencies, the perennial question of form and matter in a literary work seems to be still with us and is perhaps not altogether solved by the brief statement of the Bollingen judges. The Pound case enables us to put it to aestheticians in this definite way:

How far is it possible, in a lyric poem, for technical embellishments to transform vicious and ugly matter into beautiful poetry?

*Partisan Review,* May, 1949

# The Question of the Pound Award

by W. H. Auden
    Robert Gorham Davis
    Clement Greenberg
    Irving Howe
    George Orwell
    Karl Shapiro
    Allen Tate
    William Barrett

(Editorial Note.—We are printing below a comment on William Barrett's editorial, "A Prize for Ezra Pound," which appeared in the April issue. A number of Bollingen jurors were invited to discuss the issues connected with the award, but at the time of going to press we had received replies only from Messrs. Auden, Shapiro, and Tate. We would like to hear further from our readers on this subject.)

## W. H. AUDEN:

I fully share Mr. Barrett's concern over the excessive preoccupation of contemporary criticism with Form and its neglect of Content. I am not sure however that this is the precise problem which his comment raises. In stating my own views, I should like to emphasize that I am speaking purely for myself and am not to be construed as representing any other colleague with whom at any time I may have been associated.

1) According to one theory, art, both in intention and effect, is a means by which emotions are aroused in the spectator or reader,

either in order that, by re-living them imaginatively, he may get rid of them, or because he needs to be roused to feel in a certain way. If this theory is adopted, then it seems to me that Plato and Tolstoy are irrefutable. No works of art may be permitted which do not purge men of their bad feelings and stimulate good ones. The criterion of value may vary—Plato thought the supreme value was love of justice and loyalty to the Good State, Tolstoy thought it was love of one's neighbor—but the principle is the same. Applied to the present issue, the conclusion would be obvious—no prize; suppression.

2) One may, on the other hand, hold another theory of art, that, in intention, at least, it is a mirror in which the spectator sees reflected himself and the world, and becomes conscious of his feelings good and bad, and of what their relations to each other are in fact. This theory presupposes, I believe, certain other beliefs into which there is no time to go now, beyond baldly stating them:

a) All created existence is a good.
b) Evil is a negative perversion of created good.
c) Man has free will to choose between good and evil.
d) But all men are sinners with a perverted will.

An art which did not accurately reflect evil would not be good art.

3) This does not dispose, however, of the question of censorship. Whatever its intention, a work of art cannot compel the reader to look at it with detachment, and prevent him from using it as a stimulus to and excuse for feelings which he should condemn. Everyone, I am sure, has had the experience of reading a book which he was aware, at the time or later, was bad for him personally, whatever its artistic merit, or however harmless it might be for others, because, in this case, he was not capable of exercising free will, and was therefore not reading it as a work of art. For instance, Baudelaire's poem *La Charogne* would not be healthy reading for a necrophilist. Antisemitism is, unfortunately, not only a feeling which all gentiles at times feel, but also, and this is what matters, a feeling of which the majority of them are not ashamed. Until they are, they must be regarded as children who have not yet reached the age of consent in this matter and from whom, therefore, all books, whether works of art or not, which reflect feeling about Jews—and it doesn't make the slightest difference whether they are

pro or anti, the *New York Post* can be as dangerous as *Der Stürmer* —must be withheld.

If it were to seem likely that the *Pisan Cantos* would be read by people of this kind, I would be in favor of censoring it (as in the case of the movie, *Oliver Twist*). That would not however prevent me awarding the *Pisan Cantos* a prize before withholding it from the public. But I do not believe that the likelihood exists in this case.

## ROBERT GORHAM DAVIS:

The Pound award, it seems to me, is not most profitably taken as a problem in aesthetics. When form and content or free will and determinism or nominalism and realism are allowed to fall into this kind of abstract polarity, they can be argued about fruitlessly until doomsday. What confronts us in the Pound case is a complex of ideas dominant in American criticism during the forties, and made so largely by the talents and critical activities of some of the judges, of Eliot, Auden, Tate and Warren. The judges were judging themselves along with Pound, their master. But nearly everyone in America who is serious about literature is involved in one way or another.

The complex of ideas I speak of has been promoted with tactical skill, group movements, concerted attacks and extremes of mutual laudation. Snobbery and prestige have counted heavily. But it is not a conspiracy. There are truths in it, and much immediate support from the particular history of our time. It asserts that living language, literary sensibility and poetic values are supported by the traditional, the Catholic, the regional, the mythic, the aristocratic, and by a sense of the tragic, of transcendental absolutes, of sin and grace. Language and sensibility and values are destroyed by rationalism, liberalism, positivism, progressivism, equalitarianism, Shelleyanism, sociology, and the ideology of the Enlightenment. This has been made explicit by Eliot in *After Strange Gods* and *The Idea of a Christian Society;* by the Southern Regionalists, including Tate and Warren in much that they have written since their first manifesto, *I'll Take My Stand;* and by Auden in the Herod-as-liberal speech in *A Christmas Oratorio* and in the various reviews urging liberals and reformers to go jump in the lake.

In this complex of ideas the antisemitism with which William Barrett is principally concerned has a vital part. For these ideas did not originate with Eliot or Pound or Hulme, but with the French reactionary critics at the end of the nineteenth century, and were made into a program of action by Charles Maurras of whom Eliot used to speak with favor in *Criterion* days. Under the influence of Maurras, the virulently antisemitic students of the *Action Française* stormed the Sorbonne, beat up liberal professors, and howled down plays by Jewish writers, as untroubled as their Fascist and Nazi successors by problems of form and content. This mob antisemitism was the antisemitism of Pound's broadcasts when he, like Maurras, became a traitor both to his country and humane culture. (John Berryman's extenuating all this in PARTISAN REVIEW by comparing Pound to Roger Casement is one of the more fantastic examples of the way we are all involved.)

Eliot's antisemitism is different in kind but just as essential in his poetry and social ideas. Awed by his great achievements, fearful of showing insensibility, of introducing irrelevant "liberalism," most critics have accepted this in Eliot's terms. As homeless cosmopolitans and usurers, the Bleisteins and Sir Ferdinand Kleins represent the debasements of modern commercialism. As intellectuals, the Jews are the foremost carriers of disintegrative rationalism, earthly messianism. For the Southern Regionalists, Negroes are less interesting ideologically, but equally outside the tradition, and not to be made part of it by any liberal rhetoric.

Here we have not a question of form and content, of purity in art, but of the requirement of certain social attitudes, particularly ethical and communal ones, for literature, and rejection of certain others. These are programmatic demands, which are quite separable from the real achievements and values which they rationalize or exploit. Such demands can be refuted even by the example of many of the masters these critics claim as their own, and they are inapplicable to whole areas of literary experience which these critics undervalue or ignore. If Ezra Pound's *Cantos* are read with a wider literary and historical sense than the "new criticism" permits, they gain in meaning. As poetry they fail, despite Pound's sensibility. Their incoherence is real incoherence; it is not "achieved form." But against the author's intention they are highly revealing. They are a test case for a whole set of values, and stand self-condemned. They are important documents; they should be available, they should be read. But they deserve no prize.

## CLEMENT GREENBERG:

I agree with Mr. Barrett. The Fellows in American Letters should have said more—that is, if they had more to say, and they should have had. As a Jew, I myself cannot help being offended by the matter of Pound's latest poetry; and since 1943 things like that make me feel *physically* afraid too.

I do not quarrel here with the Fellows' aesthetic verdict, but I question its primacy in the affair at hand, a primacy that hints at an absolute acceptance of the autonomy not only of art but of every separate field of human activity. Does no hierarchy of value obtain among them? Would Mr. Eliot, for instance, approve of this for his "Christian society?"

Life includes and is more important than art, and it judges things by their consequences. I am not against the publication of *The Pisan Cantos,* even though they offend me; my perhaps irrational sensitivity as a Jew cedes to my fear of censorship in general, and to the anticipation of the pleasure to be gotten from reading poetry, and I have to swallow that consequence. But I wish the Fellows had been, or shown themselves, more aware of the additional consequence when they awarded their Bollingen Prize. They could have taken greater trouble to explain their decision and thereby spared me, and a good many Jews like me, additional offense. (This does not mean, necessarily, that I am against the award itself.)

In any case, I am sick of the art-adoration that prevails among cultured people, more in our time than in any other: that art silliness which condones almost any moral or intellectual failing on the artist's part as long as he is or seems a successful artist. It is still justifiable to demand that he be a successful human being before anything else, even if at the cost of his art. As it is, psychopathy has become endemic among artists and writers, in whose company the moral idiot is tolerated as perhaps nowhere else in society.

Although it is irrelevant to the discussion, I must not let fall the opportunity to say at this point that, long before I heard of Pound's fascist sympathies, I was struck by his chronic failure to apprehend the substance, the concrete reality, of the things he talked about or

did. I feel this failure in his poetry just as much as in what he wrote
about painting and music. As a poet he seems to me to have always
been more virtuoso than artist and to have seldom grasped the
reality of the poem as a whole, as something with a beginning,
middle, and ending. Thus, usually, any line or group of lines of a
poem by Pound impresses me as superior to the whole of which it
is part. (I would, however, except the "Mauberley" poems and
several others of the same period from this stricture.)

IRVING HOWE:

That "a poet's technical accomplishments can transform material that is ugly and vicious into beautiful poetry" is at least possible; but *how far* (as Mr. Barrett asks) he can do so I hardly
know. One thing seems certain: Pound hasn't done it. There is
nothing very beautiful in "the yidd is a stimulant," though there
is in "pull down thy vanity." Pound the crank is only rarely Pound
the poet.

Doesn't this split in Pound make possible a justification of the
Bollingen award? I think not. I would move beyond Mr. Barrett's
question and assume that the *Pisan Cantos did* contain the best
poetry of 1948. That does not yet settle the question of whether
Pound should have been given the award. For while believing in
the autonomy of aesthetic judgment, I believe in it so deeply that
I also think there are some situations when it must be disregarded.

I am against any attempt to curtail Pound's rights to publish, and
I don't want to see him prosecuted. (I don't like police measures;
and cops aren't qualified to handle poets, not even mad or fascist
poets.) I am, however, also against any campaign to condemn the
Bollingen judges. What is involved in the Pound case is not a
matter for public action but for a dialogue of conscience. But while
defending Pound's rights, I could not in good conscience acquiesce
to *honor* him with a literary award—which, if you please, must also
mean to honor him as a man.

To give Pound a literary prize is, willy-nilly, a moral act within
the frame of our social world. To honor him is to regard him as a
man with whom one can have decent, normal, even affectionately
respectful human and intellectual relations; it means to extend a
hand of public fraternity to Ezra Pound. Now a hand to help him
when he is down, yes. A hand to defend him from censors, fools and

blood-seekers, yes. But a hand of honor and congratulations, no. For Pound, by virtue of his public record and utterances, is beyond the bounds of our intellectual life. If the judges felt that he had written the best poetry of 1948, I think they should have publicly said so—but not awarded any prize for the year. That might, by the way, have been an appropriate symbol of our cultural situation.

My position has, I know, grave difficulties and can easily lead to abuse. Once you consider extra-literary matters in a literary judgment, where do you stop? You stop at the point where intelligence and sensibility tell you to—that is what they are for. But it would be absurd to deny that there are occasions when aesthetic standards and our central human values clash, and when the latter must seem more important. On such painful occasions one can only say: not that I love literature less, but that I love life more. Is there any other way of taking literature seriously?

## GEORGE ORWELL:

I think the Bollingen Foundation were quite right to award Pound the prize, if they believed his poems to be the best of the year, but I think also that one ought to keep Pound's career in memory and not feel that his ideas are made respectable by the mere fact of winning a literary prize.

Because of the general revulsion against Allied war propaganda, there has been—indeed, there was, even before the war was over—a tendency to claim that Pound was "not really" a fascist and an anti-semite, that he opposed the war on pacifist grounds and that in any case his political activities only belonged to the war years. Some time ago I saw it stated in an American periodical that Pound only broadcast on the Rome radio when "the balance of his mind was upset," and later (I think in the same periodical) that the Italian government had blackmailed him into broadcasting by threats to relatives. All this is plain falsehood. Pound was an ardent follower of Mussolini as far back as the nineteen-twenties, and never concealed it. He was a contributor to Mosley's review, the *British Union Quarterly,* and accepted a professorship from the Rome government before the war started. I should say that his enthusiasm was essentially for the Italian form of fascism. He did not seem to be very strongly pro-Nazi or anti-Russian, his real underlying motive being hatred of Britain, America and "the Jews." His broadcasts were disgusting. I remember at least one in which he approved the massacre of the East European Jews and "warned" the American Jews that their turn was coming presently. These broadcasts—I did not hear them, but only read them in the BBC monitoring report —did not give me the impression of being the work of a lunatic. Incidentally I am told that in delivering them Pound used to put on a pronounced American accent which he did not normally have, no doubt with the idea of appealing to the isolationists and playing on anti-British sentiment.

None of this is a reason for giving Pound the Bollingen Prize. There are times when such a thing might be undesirable—it would have been undesirable when the Jews were actually being killed in the gas vans, for instance—but I do not think this is one of them. But since the judges have taken what amounts to the "art for art's sake" position, that is, the position that aesthetic integrity and common decency are two separate things, then at least let us keep them separate and not excuse Pound's political career on the ground that he is a good writer. He *may* be a good writer (I must admit that I personally have always regarded him as an entirely spurious writer), but the opinions that he has tried to disseminate by means of his works are evil ones, and I think that the judges should have said so more firmly when awarding him the prize.

## KARL SHAPIRO:

Mr Barrett's analysis of the Pound award seems to be on the safe side, but his extension of the official statement of the Fellows makes it clear that we are dealing with the *pons asinorum* of modern criticism.

I voted against Pound in the balloting for the Bollingen Prize. My first and more crucial reason was that I am a Jew and cannot honor antisemites. My second reason I stated in a report which was circulated among the Fellows: "I voted against Pound in the belief that the poet's political and moral philosophy ultimately vitiates his poetry and lowers its standards as literary work." This statement of principle I would place against the official statement of the Fellows, which seems to me evasive, historically untrue, and illogical. That it was a successful device in placating opinion you know.

The newspaper editorials I saw all rejoiced in "the objective perception of value on which any civilized society must rest" and I heard one radio commentator remark benignly that "this could never happen in Russia."

What appeased the journalists must have been their belief that Pound, despite his unintelligibility to them, is on the side of beauty or "technical excellence." The Fellows and the newsmen meet at the point where an unspecified technical excellence is accepted by the lay reader as successful (i.e., "beautiful") poetry. What the journalists think would not matter very much, but Mr. Barrett follows the same line of reasoning. "How far is it possible, in a lyric poem," he asks, "for technical embellishments to transform vicious and ugly matter into beautiful poetry?" Shouldn't the question rather be: Through his experience with vicious and ugly ideas, what poetic insights into our world has this poet given us? Pound's worth as a poet rests upon some answer to such a question.

Another question is well worth asking, namely, how objective could the Fellows be in a decision of this kind? If we consider a work for literary merit alone (whatever that may mean) we imply a personal decision to disregard the mythopoeic and moral function of the artist. If Pound had sufficient intellectual honesty, he would be the first to oppose such a criterion of selection.

The jury that elected Pound was made up partly of Pound's contemporaries, those who had come under his influence as impresario and teacher, those who had at some time made declarations of political reaction, and those who had engaged in the literary struggle to dissociate art from social injunction. The presence of Mr. Eliot at the meetings gave these facts a reality which perhaps inhibited open discussion. For reasons of personal loyalty, which one must respect, and for reasons of sectarian literary loyalty, which one may or may not respect, few poets anywhere are in a position to say what they really think of Pound's work. But eventually what the serious well-intentioned critic admires in Pound is his aesthetic integrity. It is curious to see the flower of this integrity grafted onto criminality, but this should not lead us to the conclusion that artists can be criminals without incriminating their art.

The technical charge of treason against Pound is not our concern, but all artists should stand against this poet for his greater crime against civilization. Let the same charge be laid against Stalinist artists. But even if we claim to be objective perceptionists about it, let us at least ask ourselves whether fascism is or is not one of the "myths" of *The Cantos*. Who will deny that it is?

## ALLEN TATE:*

I do not propose to express any extensive views on Mr. Barrett's article, but rather to set down a brief statement of my own position on the only serious question that it raises.

A few weeks before the Bollingen Prize was awarded some persons of antisemitic feelings expressed to me their alarm lest it be given to Mr. Pound.

Mr. Barrett, it seems to me, goes a long way round, through a good deal of cant and vulgarity (to say nothing of the effrontery with which he invents the "difficulties" of the Fellows in coming to their decision), in order to arrive at the following insinuation: The decision of the Fellows in American Letters of the Library of Congress was dominated by antisemitic prejudice.

I consider any special attitude toward Jews, in so far as they may

---

* In a later issue of the *Partisan Review*, Mr. Tate discussed his reasons for voting for Pound. Among many other things he said this: "In literature as in life nothing reaches us pure. The task of the civilized intelligence is one of perpetual salvage. We cannot decide that our daily experience must be either aesthetic or practical—art of life; it is never, as it comes to us, either/or; it is always both/and. But as persons of a particular *ethos,* of a certain habit and character, we discharge our responsibilities to society from the point of view of the labors in which we are placed. We are placed in the profession of letters. We cannot expect the businessman and the politician, the men who run the state, to know that our particular responsibility exists; we cannot ask them to understand the more difficult fact that our responsibility to them is for the language which they themselves use for the general welfare. They are scarcely aware of language at all; what one is not aware of one almost always abuses. But the medium cannot be extricated from the material, the how from the what: part of our responsibility is to correct the monism of the statesman who imagines that what he says is scarcely said in language at all, that it exists apart from the medium in a "purity" of action which he thinks of a "practicality." If men of letters do not look after the medium, nobody else will. We need never fear that the practical man will fail to ignore our concern for the health of language: this he has already done by indicting Pound as if Pound, like himself, were a monist of action. Pound's language remains our particular concern. If he were a convicted traitor, I should still think that, in another direction which complicates the problem ultimately beyond our comprehension, he had performed an indispensable duty to society."

be identified as individuals or as a group, a historical calamity; and it is not less calamitous when the attitude is their own. I consider antisemitism to be both cowardly and dishonorable; I consider it cowardly and dishonorable to insinuate, as Mr. Barrett does, without candor, a charge of antisemitism against the group of writers of which I am a member.

I hope that persons who wish to accuse me of cowardice and dishonor will do so henceforth personally, in my presence, so that I may dispose of the charge at some other level than that of public discussion. Courage and honor are not subjects of literary controversy, but occasions of action.

## FURTHER COMMENT BY WILLIAM BARRETT:

I am not a Jew, but surely it must be clear to everyone by this time that antisemitism is a problem for gentiles as much as for Jews. When Jews whom I know and respect feel uneasy, as Mr. Clement Greenberg does, about a public award to Pound, I am bound to feel uneasy myself and to question the judgment of the Bollingen jury. Some of these questions I tried to raise in my brief comment. Mr. Tate's explosion in reply seems to us astonishing, to say the least. Neither Mr. Auden nor Mr. Shapiro, who were his colleagues on the Bollingen jury, have responded in his fashion; and the fact that among all the foregoing comments Mr. Tate's alone sticks out like a very sore and angry thumb is sufficient evidence that his reply was a complete and unwarranted misconstruction of my editorial, which contained absolutely no allegation whatever of antisemitism on the part of the judges. The question was, and is, the public wisdom of an award to Pound, and not the private psychology of the judges. It is Mr. Tate who has injected the personal issues. Surely Mr. Tate must recognize that he has a public responsibility to answer, not me personally, but all those people who have not forgotten what happened in Germany during this last War and who, like Mr. Greenberg, feel threatened by an award to Pound. Mr. Tate still has the opportunity open to him to offer a reasoned justification of the award, and we hope that he will do so. In the meantime, his challenge to a personal duel is strictly extra-curricular sport—having nothing to do with the public issue.

The comments explain themselves sufficiently so that it is unnecessary for me to linger in detailed examination of all of them. I should like to confine the rest of my remarks to the statements by Mr. Davis and Mr. Auden.

I agree with Mr. Davis that the context in which this question is raised has to be extended to include the historical circumstances that now condition literary judgment in the United States. What the present controversy demonstrates is that the category of the aesthetic is not the primary one for human life, and that the attitude which holds aesthetic considerations to be primary is far from primary itself, but produced by very many historical, social, and moral conditions. It would be hard to define just what the reigning climate of opinion has become in literary America since the collapse of the 'thirties; but perhaps it is high time we sought to establish a new climate, beginning with a re-examination of some of these "non-aesthetic" bases of literary judgment.

Mr. Auden's letter is the kind of rational, impersonal, and calm justification of the prize that we had hoped to have from Mr. Tate. I respect Mr. Auden's position, but I am not altogether convinced by his arguments. I would agree with everything that he says if the question had been one of censorship. But the question I raised was not one of suppressing Pound's book but of publicly honoring it with a prize. Mr. Auden's jump—"no prize; suppression"—is his own inference and not mine.

This point must be stressed since, as Mr. Shapiro remarks in his comment, some people are glad to celebrate the awards for Pound just *because* it seems a triumph of liberalism. Such is the line taken by Mr. Dwight Macdonald, who in an editorial in his magazine *Politics* finds the award "the brightest political act in a dark period." One can be in favor of the prize for Pound and still find Mr. Macdonald's enthusiasm here just a little extreme. I am against censorship in principle even though in particular cases it might be publicly beneficial, because censorship, once invoked, is difficult to control and therefore dangerous. I think this is as far as liberalism need go. To push it further is to indulge in a bohemian attitude of liberalism for liberalism's sake, which can become as unbalanced as the traditional attitude of art-for-art's sake, or of any part of life for that part's sake as abstracted from the whole. Liberalism is urged here to countenance things that deny its own right to exist—and for no other purpose but to show off. There is a kind of childishly competitive bravado in this need to show that one can out-liberal all other liberals. One step further, and Mr. Macdonald will be seeking out for a prize a *bad* poet who expresses antisemitism just in order to show how liberal he (Macdonald) can be.

Mr. Auden makes his most significant point, I think, when he argues that because evil is a part of life we have often to place great value upon works of art that do express evil attitudes. I agree with him in this, and I also agree that in his example of Baudelaire's *La Charogne* much of the power of this poem does derive from the fact that the poet participates, up to a point, in the emotions of necrophilia. For the aesthetic exploration of his subject matter the poet identifies himself with the emotions he expresses. But I doubt very much that one can call Baudelaire a necrophilist in the same public sense in which one can call Pound an antisemite. Moreover, it seems to me to make a difference that necrophilia (so far as I know) has not been connected in our time with any large political movements, necrophiliac speeches have not been broadcast over the radio, and there are not large numbers of decent people who feel that their lives are threatened by necrophilists. Thus Mr. Orwell's remarks about Pound's broadcasts do not seem irrelevant to the present problem: the antisemitic lines I quoted from *The Pisan Cantos* simply versify statements made by Pound in his broadcasts to the effect that the War was brought about by the Jews, for whose interests American soldiers were being killed like cattle. In comparison, necrophilia still remains a private evil.

Since the discussion has unfortunately brought out some acrimony, I am glad to resign my part in it on at least one note of unqualified admiration—and that is for Mr. Karl Shapiro's comment, which is the kind of courageous and outspoken statement that has become a rare thing on our literary scene. I would agree with Mr. Shapiro that he has made a much better statement of the question of form and content in a literary work than I did in my comment. I also think with him that fascism is part of the "myth" of the *Cantos* generally—and that it can be found in *The Pisan Cantos* too.

# Excerpts from a Journal: 1949

by RAY WEST

*February 22.* The newspapers announced today that Ezra Pound had won the first Bollingen Prize in Poetry. The account (under an A.P. dateline on the front page) was highly editorialized and full of such epithets as "mad poet," "fascist traitor," etc. I think most journalists are pleased to see Pound publicly humiliated—or any serious poet. Pound's influence during the past forty years has been tremendous. One could see his influence in the James revival and in the recognition of Joyce. Few people realize how much of Pound is in Eliot, even though Eliot acknowledged the critical influence in the pages of *Poetry* a few years ago.

*February 23.* The newspaper editorialized the Pound award today. The same charges. I believe it was Malcolm Cowley who wrote, just after Pound had been pronounced insane, that it was unfortunate that Pound had not been allowed to stand trial. As a man, he could then have been punished or exonerated; the nature and extent of his guilt or innocence would have been determined by the court. As a poet, he is on trial only for the quality of his poetry, and to like his work does not necessarily imply a liking for his economic or political views.

*March 3.* Just read through *The Case of Ezra Pound* (Charles Norman, The Bodley Press). Sometime ago I read *If This Be Treason,* a pamphlet put out by Olga Rudge in Italy, containing several of Pound's broadcasts. Those broadcasts were full of the

67

familiar Pound eccentricities, but aside from anti-British sentiments they were non-political—on such subjects as E. E. Cummings, Joyce, etc. This book by Norman also has excerpts from
the broadcasts, and in at least one of them Pound's anti-Semitism
seems quite clear. Yet Louis Zukofsky writes: "I never felt the
least trace of anti-Semitism in his presence." To say Pound's anti-
Semitism was ideological or mythical does not excuse it, but it may
help to explain the man. No one that I know considers Pound
correct in his thinking. The chief weakness in his work (especially
in his prose) grows from the bad taste, perhaps the pose, which
resulted in a good deal of bad writing and which obscured his
occasional very fine insights. Certainly there is no anti-Semitism
in "Brennbaum," one of the *Hugh Selwyn Mauberly* sequences.
Note the last stanza:

> The heavy memories of Horeb, Sinai and the forty years,
> Showed only when the daylight fell
> Level across the face
> Of Brennbaum "The Impeccable."

The irony here is the irony of "Sweeney" and "Prufrock," and I believe Eliot learned it from Pound.

*April 10.* I read today "The Case of Ezra Pound" in P.R. A
short article by William Barrett criticizes the Fellows for making
the award to Pound. Its tone is belligerent, even nasty, heavily
sarcastic. It does raise a legitimate question, but one not completely
neglected in the announcement of the award, as to how far it is
possible, ". . . in a lyric poem, for technical embellishments to
transform vicious and ugly matter into beautiful poetry?" The
quotation displays a bias, but the question deserves an answer.
A poem with "technical embellishments" is a bad poem. The word
"embellishments" obscures B.'s real question. The question, I take
it, is, can one be even mildly anti-Semitic and write a successful
(beautiful) poem about a Jew? I hope I shall not be accused of
anti-Semitism if I answer, yes. I should prefer to have the anti-
Semitism of our age (and who will deny that it exists?) written
from a point of view contrary to Pound's, just as I should have
preferred it if Eliot had not joined the Church, if Huxley had not
become converted to mysticism, if Andre Malraux had not become

a DeGaullist, if Breton had not become a communist, and if William Faulkner had not so bitterly resented the Civil Rights Bill. The fact that we feel strongly about anyone who is anti-Semitic, makes it difficult for us to evaluate the treatment of it as subject matter. Who knows, even, that we are judging Pound correctly as a man? I am at least as impressed by what Louis Zukofsky writes about his relationship with Pound as I am by the word (and it is an ugly word) "Kike" used in the Cantos. I recognize an opposite danger, such as that suggested by an editor who considers Melville's attitude toward the Negro in *Benito Cereno* as questionable. The use of the Negro in this novel does not indicate that Melville was anti-Negro. The problem simply did not exist for him. He was using a conventional symbol which was, to be sure, ugly, but so much of literature deals with the ugly. In fact, Pound comments upon the problem in *Canto LXXX:*

> La beauté, "Beauty is difficult, Yeats" said Aubrey
> Beardsley
> > when Yeats asked why he drew horrors
> > or at least not Burne-Jones
> > and Beardsley knew he was dying and had to
> > make his hit quickly

Hence no more B-J in his product.

*May 15.* The May issue of P.R. arrived a few days ago. Most depressing reading! Sidney Hook's article "Reflections on the Jewish Question" is very good, but coming as it does in an issue containing eight letters on the Pound question, it cannot be read without recognizing the tremendous emotional pressures involved (naturally enough, but nevertheless tragic) in the whole question. Hook writes:

> According to Sartre the man of democratic principle, although a better person than the antisemite, is just as hostile to the Jew as a Jew. He wants him to disappear into the abstract universal, *man,* and annihilate himself as a concrete, historical individual. Whereas the antisemite "wishes to destroy the Jew as a man and leave nothing in him but the Jew, the Pariah, the untouchable."

Hook believes that each man should have the right to exist as he chooses, "as Jews or Gentiles, as citizens of one country or another, as cultural heirs of Socrates or Aquinas or Dewey." With this I agree, although I must admit that I am troubled by Jews who attempt to hide their Jewishness, just as I am troubled by Mormons who do not take a certain pride in their origins. This is not a sentimental attitude. The individual retains, then, the right to criticize, to point out what seems to him false in his tradition.

In these terms I respect the statements of Clement Greenberg and Karl Shapiro, without, however, agreeing with them. Robert Gorham Davis's position troubles me most. He opposes the award because he seems to recognize in it a latent fascism and anti-Semitism as represented in the membership of the Fellows. This is an absurd charge, and it is rendered with a particular arrogance which the committee members would have reason to resent. He refers directly only to Eliot as anti-Semitic, but includes the others (and presumably a good many others) as represented by a "complexity of ideas" which ". . . asserts that living language, literary sensibility and poetic values are supported by the traditional, the Catholic, the regional, the mythic, the aristocratic, and by a sense of the tragic, or transcendental absolutes, or sin and grace." This is indeed a complexity, and one wonders what remains for Mr. D.'s good life (and art) except a simplicity which would, like Plato's, banish the poet forever from society.

The implications of D.'s position are, however, most frightening, and suggest those aspects of Plato which have been called fascistic. There are usually three steps in the process which D. suggests: (1) you decide what is true (D.'s tone implies a certain knowledge of the truth); (2) you discountenance all other views, first by ridicule and smear (as in D.'s article), then by edict; (3) you punish all persons associating with those who hold such views (you do not read Pound, Eliot, Tate, or Warren, to choose Mr. D.'s examples).

This last is the book-burning stage, and while D. would undoubtedly say he does not countenance such extremes, the ideology which he represents has prepared the way for it in our age both in Germany and in Russia.

*June 9.* T. was here for dinner last night. Much talk about the Bollingen Award. Today a phone call from Washington told of a new attack on it in S.R.L. Ironically, the author is Robert Hillyer, whose appointment to the faculty at Kenyon had just been the topic of conversation. No copy to be had as yet.

*June 12.* Saw a copy of S.R.L. in the library. Hillyer's attack (titled "Treason's Strange Fruit") is illogical, bad-tempered, and scurrilous, much worse than D.'s in P.R. It not only condemns the award (every person's right), but H. sees a conspiracy of poets, critics, psychoanalysts, publishers, and god-knows-what-all under the banner of obscurity in poetry, religio-mythology, and the New Criticism. (Here are D's complexities become more complex.) This article should thoroughly confuse the issues of the Pound award. Even if the editors of S.R.L. do not claim to be publishing a literary magazine (and I believe they do), this would be irresponsible publishing.

*August 25.* I am on vacation and out of touch, but a note in the newspaper announces that the Bollingen Award has been withdrawn.

*October 20.* Asked to sign a letter circulated by John Berryman objecting to the manner of attack employed by H. and addressed to the editor and publisher of S.R.L. The letter says:

> The literary and political values of the poetry of Ezra Pound offer wide latitudes of support and opposition, as all poetry does in one degree or another. Discussion of the Bollingen award in these terms is to be welcomed.
>
> But the methods employed by Robert Hillyer in the recent attacks published in your pages (June 11 and 18) and supported by your several editorials, are in our opinion reprehensible, in the following terms:
>
> Under the pretense of attacking the award of the Bollingen Prize to Ezra Pound, you sanctioned and guided a prepared attack on modern poetry and criticism, impugning not only the literary reputations but the personal characters of some of its foremost writers. In the blanket attack you included persons not connected with the award in any capacity, as well as its donor. Through the technique of the smear and of "guilt by association" you linked the names of T. S. Eliot, Ezra Pound, Paul Mellon, and Carl Jung, and adumbrated a Fascist conspiracy, for which you did not produce the evidence, and by implication you included in this attack not only certain of the Fellows in

American Letters of the Library of Congress, but also a larger group of unnamed writers who were participating in the "conspiracy." We submit that public decency, to say nothing of personal honor—two indispensable standards of democratic action—required you, in view of the gravity of the charges, to name specifically all the accused persons. Considering the number of printed retractions and apologies in subsequent issues of your journal, we are forced to believe that your critical examination of the validity of Robert Hillyer's allegations, before you published them, was somewhat less than disinterested, and that thus your campaign was conducted in a dangerous and unprincipled manner.

I signed the letter with pleasure!

*November 2.* Received a copy of the booklet *The Case Against the Saturday Review of Literature* (published by *Poetry*). It contains statements by a committee of the Fellows, by Allen Tate, Leonie Adams, and Luther Evans; also reprints by Malcolm Cowley, Haydn Carruth, Aline B. Louchheim, and the editors of the Hudson Review; also letters by Archibald MacLeish, Mark Van Doren, William Meredith, William Van O'Connor, Cleanth Brooks, and Yvor Winters. Included with it was a copy of the letter from Berryman, signed by seventy-three persons, including Newton Arvin, R. P. Blackmur, Richard Chase, E. E. Cummings, Francis Fergusson, Wallace Fowlie, Joseph Frank, Stanley Edgar Hyman, Randall Jarrell, Alfred Kazin, Harry Levin, Arthur Mizener, J. F. Powers, Philip Rahv, I. A. Richards, Mark Schorer, Delmore Schwartz, Donald Stauffer, Peter Taylor, Glenway Wescott, and Stark Young.

*December 1.* A letter from T. today. "The S.R.L. has double-talked for two weeks trying to get out of publishing the letter. We are withdrawing it. Margaret Marshall will print it in the Nation on December 17. Smith made unreal conditions, such as: he was entitled to know the names of the persons not signing; he needed to know about previous attempts to 'collect signatures' (there were none), etc. John Berryman gave him yesterday as a deadline . . ."

*December 4.* A letter from H.S. of S.R.L. today. A note attached says: "We are enclosing a copy of a letter sent to Mr. Berryman in reply to a peremptory telegram demanding publication of his petition, to which your name is attached." The letter repeats the request to know the names of those refusing to sign, shows reluctance to continue the controversy, but ends: "If you will agree to our request, we have a letter in reply from Robert Hillyer ready for immediate publication."

The final copy of the Berryman letter has eleven additional signers, including Lionel Trilling, Austin Warren, William Troy, Josephine Miles, and Louis Kronenberger, making a total of eighty-four names. Is one submitting a letter of this kind obligated to name those not replying? Who knows for what reason they did not sign, or to what use their names might be put?

It is time now to forget S.R.L. and let it expire in peace. P.R. raised genuine questions, though the raising of them might have been left to a more capable person than W.B. The question of Pound's sanity has presumably been settled by government medical men; the question of treason must await judgment from the courts. Pound's personal beliefs and prejudices are open to question, and it must not be assumed that everyone who reads his poetry shares them. The immediate job, insofar as it is possible, should be a serious evaluation of the poetry, particularly the *Pisan Cantos*. Two magazines now contemplate Pound issues (*Quarterly* Review of Literature and the Hudson Review); perhaps they will assist in estimating not only Pound's value as a poet and critic, but also his limitations.

*The New York Times,* September 4, 1949*

# The State and Art

by ALINE LOUCHHEIM SAARINEN

Following the bitter controversy over the award of the $1,000 Bollingen Prize in Poetry to Ezra Pound by the Fellows in American Letters of the Library of Congress, the Library has announced the cancellation of all its prizes in literature, music, and art.

The decision is of interest to the art world on two counts. One, it means there will be no prizes in the J. and E. R. Pennell annual print exhibition ("The National Exhibition of Prints"). From the point of view of monetary rewards, the effect of the stop-order is negligible as there are only three $100 prizes. But in terms of the prestige which these prizes carry, their cancellation is disheartening to print-makers. Two, the principles involved touch on the larger questions of the position of advanced forms of expression in all the arts in America and of the relation of government to the arts.

It is not within our sphere to take sides for or against the Fellows' judgment in citing the *Pisan Cantos* by Ezra Pound (who has not only been indicted for treason but has also been judged insane). But the questions of whether the Government should single out individual works for award and of who should make this selection do concern the art world.

The Librarian chose the personnel of the jury from the Library's large group of literary advisers because he believed them competent to make aesthetic and scholarly judgment in poetry. Our colleagues

---

* Reprinted in *The Case Against SRL,* 39-42.

in the literary field confirm the respected position of this personnel. Although he personally disagreed with the jury, Librarian Luther Evans remarked in a letter to the Saturday Review of Literature: "The American people are assumed to wish for a free and full development of their cultural life. It would not be to the interest of such development if members of a professional advisory committee were to falsify their opinions in order to escape censure or to make a popular choice."

But apparently Mr. Evans is overestimating the American people and their Government. In clarifying the decree which ordered the cancellation of the literary prize, Senator Theodore Green, Chairman of the joint Senate-House Library committee, told this reporter: "We are opposed to the Government discriminating between individuals in the matter of taste. There are no standards to apply, only personal opinions. A Library of Congress prize carries the prestige of all the people and if its prizes do not represent all the people, the Government is bound to get into trouble."

Presumably, if it could stay out of "trouble" by pleasing everybody the Government might, in its encouragement of the arts, single out special achievement for honorable mention. But it is apparently not proper for the Government to use specialist-consultants to designate these achievements lest their decisions offend and anger.

In other words, the "everybody" or the "common man" in this century of the C. M. is apparently as qualified as a distinguished critic or an eminent artist to pass aesthetic judgment. We are back at the criteria of excellence voiced today with such alarming frequency: intelligibility and style to suit the lowest common denominator of taste—despite the fact that a work of art is not a common but a peculiarly *un*common thing. True, poets and painters and musicians and critics may occasionally make erroneous judgment, but does that refute the correctness, the desirability, perhaps even the necessity, of calling upon them to render a service of selection for the Government? And, granting a few misguided decisions, isn't the special achievement award exactly the kind of recognition which a government interested in encouraging the arts should give?

By its retreat it might appear that the Library itself is opposed

to government awards and itself denies that the intellectual and
scholarly elite should serve as government representatives. Many
of our readers have so interpreted the recent action, branding it
"intellectual cowardice" and "Chamberlain appeasement."

But other interpretations are possible. It is clear that public
censure in the form of disagreement with the jury was not what
provoked the prize cancellation. The Library recognizes the democratic right of anyone to take issue with the jury's choice.

What was disturbing was that many of the attacks were aimed
at the jury because it was a body favoring advanced modes of expression and that many of the antagonists tried to denigrate the
jury personnel by insinuation and association. Presumably this
kind of attack inspired the threat of Congressional investigation—
and an investigation, in turn, seemed to mean that the principle of
a jury of "intellectual peers" might be abandoned in favor of a
future compromising, popularly—perhaps even politically-minded
jury.

The Library would prefer no prizes to such a compromise.
Moreover, the Library has splendidly encouraged the arts. Especially in music and dance it has sponsored progressive work which
might otherwise not have had a hearing. Although the awards
have usually been on the conservative side, the annual print exhibitions have shown advanced as well as traditional graphic work.
Although it will abandon awards, the Library will continue its
sponsorship of the arts with concerts, exhibitions, and purchases.
Thus, the retreat on the prize issue may perhaps be understood as
the small concession necessary to preserve the greater service.

Such attitudes will be characterized as "defeatist." But many
people who have long hoped for vital and far-reaching Government
sponsorship of the arts are also defeatist. The memory of the
shameful fate of the "State Department pictures" is still vivid.
Currently Congressman Dondero is waging a campaign against
modern art, using with ugly finesse every unpleasant technique,
calling it Communist and smearing artists by insinuation and association. Although the fallacies of his syllogistic reasoning could
be spotted by a student in freshman logic, the temper of our times
makes his twisted conclusions popular.

Certainly it is better to relinquish a fight for Government sponsorship of art than to acquiesce to the Dondero-aesthetics, which, to quote from an article in the September *Harper's,* are: "Art which does not portray our beautiful country in plain, simple terms that everyone can understand breeds dissatisfaction. It is therefore opposed to our Government, and those who create and promote it are our enemies."

Perhaps the charge of intellectual cowardice should be levelled at those persons concerned with the arts who allow such voices as Dondero's to "represent" them in Congress.

# Ezra Pound, Traitor and Poet

by EARLE DAVIS

Ezra Pound, American citizen, adjudged a traitor to his country in World War II, is still considered America's greatest poet in the twentieth century by a remarkable number of literary critics. His influence upon T. S. Eliot, James Joyce, and Ernest Hemingway emphasizes a reputation which is founded upon numberless contradictions in fact and opinion. His violent criticism of everything from modern education to capitalist democracy, from stupid mediocrity to stodgy scholarship, stamps him as a controversial figure in any age. Consider his remarkable life story.

Born in Idaho, Pound received the usual American college education, specialized in modern languages, took a master's degree in Spanish at the University of Pennsylvania, and went out to Wabash College in Indiana to begin a teaching career. An extraordinary individualist with a capacity for not getting along with people (examine his later statement in a letter to Wyndham Lewis, "There's only one thing to do with an Englishman—kick him in the teeth"), he found the rigors of American teaching very trying, got himself dismissed summarily, and went to Europe to get a doctorate. The prospect of writing a thesis upon the verb in Lope de Vega's plays led him to give up teaching as a career.

His growing interest in the creation of poetry led him to stay in London where he supported himself precariously. His abilities rapidly made him a major figure in the revolutionary modern movement in literature and the arts. He left America in 1905. He moved to Italy in 1922. He visited briefly in America in the late thirties when his father died. He came back for the last time when the Americans caught him in North Italy after the collapse of Germany. He came back as a traitor, having broadcast from Italy against his native country. He was never tried for his treason, but was placed in a "hospital" for the mentally unbalanced, being judged "unaccountable on psychological grounds for his collaboration with the enemy." He is still officially accounted insane, but his last published poems, the *Pisan Cantos,* won the Bollingen Award in 1949 for the best poetry written by an American since the war.[1] The Bollingen Award was given from the Library of Congress, implying a kind of official American accolade, and the ensuing literary argument about making a traitor a kind of American poet laureate actually put poetry into several headlines and the news.

The interest of the general public in poetry is a limited and specialized interest. Perhaps poetry has always been an art form which appeals primarily to an intellectual class, and in the twentieth century poetry has become more and more the property of a coterie of intellectuals. After Pound's capture, the attitude of the intellectuals who have made modern poetry their own possession was that Pound was still the man who had done more than anyone else to establish whatever is distinctive about the twentieth century poetic manner. Embarrassed by his traitorous conduct, they talked about the fact that poetry and life are two different states of being, and whatever one thinks of Pound's ideas in politics, his poetic accomplishment is great enough to overcome the eventual fact of his treason.

There are several points to be made with reference to the remarkable Pound story. One can only begin to document these points. The first one is that the praise of Pound's poetry after the fact of his treason makes the whole case for modern poetry suspect to the general public, whatever the critics may say. A second point is that a special award to Pound for poems written in a prison camp

---

[1] *The Pisan Cantos* are numbered 74-84 and are part of the long poem, the *Cantos,* which is devoted to many themes besides politics and economics. However, these Pisan poems do concentrate particularly on Pound's reactions to his experiences following his capture, and they certainly show no compromise with his earlier opinion.

after his capture and after he has been declared insane indicates that modern critics like to praise the kind of poetry which is not necessarily connected with reason.

Let us imagine that we are not critics with a special knowledge of poetry. We are reasonably literate and are interested in good writing. Our natural attitude is to believe that any modern writer is attempting to say something which we can understand if we have sufficient information. Pound himself has repeatedly said that poetry is concentrated meaning, that poets are the antennae of the race, that they say more than common men say. The strange result of America's awarding a laurel wreath to Pound's *Pisan Cantos* becomes even more strange when we consider that in these poems Pound was attacking America and what we fought for in the war. Granted that our war aims may not have been clear to all of us. But look at what Pound was saying. His opinions include a strong belief that Mussolini was still right, that the last war was like all others, that the Farben cartels are still in business, that America is still controlled by evil big business, that Roosevelt was a "spotted lambe" both black and white, that Churchill was a "sputtering tank of nicotine and stale whiskey," that Socialist England was a step in the right direction of good government, and that our democracy has completely failed in acquiring what John Adams and Thomas Jefferson visualized for it.

These opinions illuminate, if they do not wholly explain Pound's treason. Many Americans differ about a definition of democracy, and we have little difficulty in avoiding broadcasting for Mussolini. The fact of the matter is that the Bollingen Award would not have been given to Pound had it not been for his earlier poetry. George Dillon, editor of *Poetry* magazine, dismisses Pound's latter opinions as "political balderdash." T. S. Eliot, after confessing that his monumental *Wasteland* was printed after Pound pruned and cut it into its present form, confesses that he continually disagrees with Pound's ideas; but the poetic manner still fascinates him. He says: "There is nobody living who can write like this; how many can be named, who can write as well?" Allen Tate, probably the most hypercritical of the modern higher critics of modern poetry, says: "Pound's Cantos are not about anything, but they are distinguished poetry."

One cannot ignore the fact that there is much mixed thinking and a great deal of ignorance in these typical opinions, despite the genius of several of these critics. The case for poetry on any level is not assisted by assuming that writing means nothing, even if it is poetry. Pound's poetry is writing. Such an absurdly simple statement ought not to be necessary. From 1905 to the present, Pound wrote poems which epitomize modern poetic tendencies. He first attempted to recreate in English the subject matter and the techniques of the best poetry written through the centuries by the greatest poets of other lands and times. He imitated and revisualized in English the finest writing of the Greeks, the Latins, the Trouba-dours, the Chinese, Japanese, Italians, French, and Germans. He gave the original spark to the Imagist movement. He tried to make words beautiful and expressive of the highest sentiments and emotions possible to our language. His ideals are easily praised in the direction of technical perfection.

To say that technique is all is to insult Pound. It is his greatest tragedy that his admirers have misunderstood him. He perfected his conception of technique to the point that not only does he seem in-comprehensible to the general public, but his adherents concentrate upon his technique and not upon what he tried to do with his technical effects. Pound was fascinated by the Chinese "character," the letters or words which originally were pictures of what the characters meant. He was fascinated by the French symbolists, who said that to suggest meaning was better than saying it outright. He was fascinated by something which has often been called *im-pressionism,* where the implied background of meaning stands for a greater whole of reference and thought.

His background of study in many languages and poets led him in his *Cantos* to a manner which is a hodge-podge of many techniques. He flickers from idea to idea, from reference to refer-ence, from quotation to quotation. He changes perspective con-stantly, like a motion picture camera. Just as one catches a reference which means something, just as one begins to appreciate a certain way of writing, he shifts to something else. Like the Milton he despised, he lies about in splendid fragments.

Critics of late have decided to explain his technique by saying that he assumes a mask (his collected early poems are entitled

*Personae,* that is, masks). In the manner of the dramatic monologue derived from his admiration for Browning he thinks poetically in a form of stream of consciousness, combining references to history, philosophy, poetry, politics, and economics with his own personal focus of emphasis. He never explains the focus, and the reader must be familiar with the point of reference before he sees the point of the accumulated materials.

The best way for the average student to understand Pound is to assume that he was writing puzzles in poetic form. A reference to Catullus becomes completely clear in most cases if one looks up the proper place in Catullus. A reference to John Adams may demand the reading of all twenty-eight volumes of Adams, but comprehension will follow. Pound was indubitably a scholar. He read so widely that his reading became interlocked with his kind of writing. One can only suspect that critics like Allen Tate and Yvor Winters are unable to understand Pound's scholarship or else they lack comprehension of what Pound was trying to accomplish. Judge from Tate's remark, "There is no reason to infer that Mr. Pound knows in the least what he is doing or saying." If Mr. Tate were not one of the most respected of modern critics, the quotation would be absurd.

There is no time in an essay of this kind to show all the things Pound was doing and saying in the *Cantos.* Let the one special field which bears upon his treason illuminate the issue. Pound has devoted himself since 1920 exclusively to his epic poem, the *Cantos.* There are eighty-two of them now; he once set a goal of a hundred.[2] In the *Cantos* Pound developed his political philosophy.

What exactly is this political philosophy? All articles on Pound avoid it like the plague. At best, they say it is a form of socialism. Actually, Pound's beliefs derive from a radical economic philosophy. He believes that the perfect government must be based upon state control of money and banking, and that there is no practical way of getting control of the economic life of the state for the good of all people except through a dictator, a brainy man who will

---

[2] Technically there were 84 at this date (1951). Two cantos remain unpublished (72 and 73), supposedly because they state Pound's position flatly, and he felt that this was hardly the time to put them in print. Since 1951 Pound has published *Section: Rock-Drill, Cantos* 85-95 (1956).

use his power for the general good. Specifically this economic philosophy has been expounded in print by Douglas, Gesell, and Orage (the only books by Gesell in English were privately printed in Dallas, generally unavailable now). These economists are considered crackpot extremists by every economist who possesses an American reputation. In a sense, the idea of controlling the economic life of the state through a strong central government is akin to the theory of the present British Labor Party. But Pound goes much farther.

Because terms like socialism and communism may be used loosely, one needs to be reminded that Pound is an individualist. He is violently opposed to communism, since communism violates individualism. Pound wants every man praised and paid for his just deserts in work and production. He objects to American capitalist democracy because he says that people who produce in America are not rewarded in proportion to their worth. Under the American free enterprise system, we have developed what Veblen called a "leisure class" society where money and work and production are disconnected. One makes money today by luck, by manipulating money, not by producing. This type of argument allowed Pound to become a fanatical adherent of Mussolini because he believed that Mussolini was trying to set up a socialist corporate state which would permit men to make money by producing something.

Even this brief statement of Pound's political and economic beliefs is a key to a great number of the *Cantos*. He continually refers to Jefferson, John Adams, and Martin Van Buren, implying that their philosophy was similar to Mussolini's. He examines the history of banks and the growth of economy dependent upon interest, coupons, dividends, profits, and usury. He spends much time in a rather dull recounting of the history of China, since Chinese history gives the best model for the understanding of all history in that it is more complete than any other nation's and therefore illustrates what can happen to any nation. Pound seized upon various men who were ideal dictators—men like Jefferson and Adams, Confucius (this "hero" is apparently a talker rather than a doer), the little-known Chinese ruler Ouang-Ngan-chè, Sigismondo Malatesta (an Italian prince of the time of the Borgias),

Pietro Leopoldo Ferdinando (the only good Hapsburg), Mussolini, and others. To make the case for Mussolini clear, he published in 1933 a book entitled *Jefferson and/or Mussolini,* attempting to show in detail how Mussolini was trying to do in Italy what Jefferson had done in America for democracy.

Two brief quotations will illustrate the best side of his arguments, and these quotations come from *Cantos* LXI and XLIV. Of Ouang-Ngan-chè, Pound says that this Chinese hero promoted a state where prices were set, where a market tax paid all government expenses, where the government insured an easy standard of living, low prices, and generally stimulated commerce and business on the basis of distribution and service to the people:

> IN time of common scarcity; to sell at the just price in extraordinary let it be lent to the people and in great calamities, give it free. . . .

Leopoldo is the kind of benevolent ruler who:

> wished state debt brought to an end;
> that put the guilds under common tribunal;
>   [that is, who made the labor unions subservient
>   to government and national interest]
> that left names only as vestige of feudal chain;
> that lightened mortmain that princes and church be under tax
>     as were others; that ended the gaolings for debt;
> that said thou shalt not sell public offices;
> that suppressed so many *gabelle;*
>   [*gabelle,* a salt tax, suggests apparently the special
>   taxes for the benefit of some special interest or
>   industry]
> that freed the printers of surveillance and wiped out the crime
>     of lèse majesty;
> that abolished death as a penalty and all tortures in prisons
>     which he held were for segregation;
> that split common property among tillers;
> roads, trees, and the wool trade,
> the silk trade, and a set price, lower, for salt. . . .

Mussolini as an issue is dead and gone. That Pound interpreted him as a socially-minded benevolent dictator who was setting up an ideal democracy seems to many Americans to be evidence of insanity. Yet Pound was not a Lord Haw-Haw, nor yet a male Tokyo Rose. He did not become involved directly in the killing of American soldiers. He broadcast theory. He had lived long in Italy. He had certainly lost any sense of patriotism, if he ever had any. Yet he refers to Hitler in the seventy-second *Canto* in a manner which indicates that he felt there was complete difference between the aims of Mussolini and Hitler. He shows equal dislike of Jewish bankers and concentration-camp tortures. Maybe he was so mixed up that a mental hospital is the proper punishment for him.

The end of the Pound story is not yet in sight, of course. Other poets in world history have been traitorous and eventually held up to fame and glory. Dante was a traitor to Florence. Shelley and Byron exiled themselves from Britain and wrote violently about their native land and the English system of government. That England never went to war with Italy in those days perhaps saved them from any act of treason that could be punished officially. We study Dante, Shelley, and Byron with varying degrees of respect and admiration today. How about the flamboyant, red-haired, exuberant, overbearing, egocentric, headline-hunting, superintellectual, mad Ezra Pound?

It is not my purpose to attack the political philosophy of Ezra Pound. Most readers can get some idea of their reaction to his ideas even by way of sketchy recapitulation here. But remember that the strangest part of the Pound story is that perfectly good American apologists have concentrated upon ignoring his message, his ideas, his philosophy. They have praised him because he wrote "great poetry."

I often wonder what the lovers of Pound will do when they come to grips with the essence of his poetry—with what he preached. There are many Americans who believe in different interpretations of the idea of democracy. There are many great writers who have been critical of some part of our way of life. Some of these writers, like Henry James and T. S. Eliot, have turned their backs upon American citizenship. The question is: can Pound's position as an American poet, his place as a great writer be disconnected from his political philosophy? Robert Penn Warren once said that great poets mean what they say. Pound also said it over the radio.[3]

I once knew a brilliant musician who was intelligent and cultured in many fields. His favorite poet was Carl Sandburg. Since his own political philosophy was an extreme of economic royalism, he was also an old-fashioned Republican of the Harding-Coolidge era. I pointed out to him that his own views and those of Carl Sandburg were at some variance. But like most intelligent readers of poetry, he had never bothered with what the poet was talking about. Only when he spent an evening in Sandburg's company did he suddenly come to understand. Then he went home and threw all Sandburg's books out of the window of his ninth-story apartment.

I admit sympathy for those who like Pound's poetry. It is a scholar's poetry, even if it annoys many scholars. It is a poet's poetry, even if some poets praise the manner rather than the matter. There are moments when one who reads Pound gets that flash of exaltation which accompanies the greatest writing in any language. That there is thunder of an ominous sound after the lightning is a tribute to Pound's genius. Nor do I believe that Pound is any more mad now than he has ever been. Modern critics may make the most of his insanity.

---

[3] Pound's broadcasts from Italy were monitored and are procurable from the *Library of Congress* in printed form: *Transcripts of Shortwave Broadcasts From Rome:* December 7, 1941-July 25, 1942. The amazing thing about these transcripts is that they are devoted to the same kind of literary form which often distinguishes Pound's critical writing, and are very difficult to understand on any terms. Several of them explicate certain Cantos, making what Pound said in the Cantos even more difficult to interpret. One can hardly blame the authorities for dodging a trial in which this material would have to be presented to a jury as proving treason. In fact, as broadcasts, these transcripts are generally unbelievable.

From Archibald MacLeish, *Poetry and Opinion,*
*The Pisan Cantos of Ezra Pound,*
(Urbana: University of Illinois Press, 1950)

# Poetry and Opinion

by ARCHIBALD MACLEISH

Editors' note: Mr. MacLeish's dialogue is a debate between Mr.
Saturday, or the Saturday Review of Literature, and Mr. Bollingen,
or the point of view held by the committee that awarded the Bollingen
Prize to Ezra Pound. Mr. MacLeish says that every generation has
debated the function of poetry, from Plato down to the present. The
passages reprinted here are from the closing pages of the book.

*Mr. Saturday:* You are thinking of Aristotle's conclusion that the
function of poetry—at least of poetic tragedy—is to reveal the underlying coherence of life?

*Mr. Bollingen:* His conclusion that poetry is an instrument of
knowledge. Which, in his time, revealed the underlying
coherence which life then had.

*Mr. Saturday:* And you consider that Pound's *Pisan Cantos* reveal
the underlying coherence of life in our day? Is fascism the
underlying coherence of our experience of life?

*Mr. Bollingen:* Is it fascism that the *Pisan Cantos* "reveal" or is it
Pound's conception of the decay of civilization in the
generations since the industrial revolution and the rise of
finance capitalism?

*Mr. Saturday:* The fascism is there. The whole poem is rotten with
it.

87

*Mr. Bollingen:* It is there. But is it there for its own sake or to define and emphasize Pound's contempt for what he calls "usuria"—the economy, the society, he thinks he sees and is sure he hates?

*Mr. Saturday:* If you mean to ask whether the purpose of the poem is to convert me to fascism or to disgust me with my own time and my own country—which happen to be Mr. Pound's as well—I should agree that the purpose is to disgust me. Does that improve the poem?

*Mr. Bollingen:* Let me go back to Aristotle for a moment. If poetry is an instrument of knowledge of a certain kind—knowledge about our lives—intuitive knowledge of the kind neither reason nor science is able to supply—then what is the poet's duty? To reveal to us what is? Or to reveal what ought to be?

*Mr. Saturday:* He can only "reveal" what exists. If he presents "what ought to be" he is trying to teach.

*Mr. Bollingen:* And if he is to reveal what exists, should he reveal what he himself believes to exist, or what common opinion assumes to exist, or what the dominant ideas of the time and place declare must exist?

*Mr. Saturday:* If poetry is an instrument of intuitive perception, what he himself perceives. Or thinks he does.

*Mr. Bollingen:* And if what he thinks he perceives is a vast disorder; a confused, bewildered, materialistic civilization running blindly and without dignity or faith upon vulgarity and death; a generation lost to its past and its future, to beauty and to grace;—if the coherence he perceives is this *in*-coherence, is it not precisely this his work must reveal?

*Mr. Saturday:* As it is precisely this by which his work must be judged. If perception is the business of the poet then it is by the justness of his perceptions that his poems must be measured.

*Mr. Bollingen:* You seem to imply that because Pound's perception of our time and place is contemptuous of both it must lack

justness. But is that true? From Baudelaire on down, poetry
has thought it saw in our industrial civilization not an
eternal, or even a temporal, order, but a tragic disorder
which made meaningless the very heart of meaning. Some
poets, it is true, used the art of poetry as Rimbaud used it
to press through the disorder and incoherence to an experience of private rapture which a worldly and ambitious
church was unable either to give or to remember. Others,
like Yeats, used the art to erect, beyond fear and beyond
faith and beyond remorse, the tower of a stoical and tragic
joy. Others still, like Mallarmé, attempted, by the incarna-
tion of the metaphor, to construct a paradise safe even from
the hopes of men. But few poets of our age indeed, and
they by no means the greatest, considered that it lay within
the honest practice of their art to present the central meaning of our time in terms of order and of beauty and of virtue.
Loyalty to the art of poetry has not been synonymous, in
other words, with loyalty to the society and the values it
accepts.

*Mr. Saturday:* But *dis*loyalty to these values! Disloyalty to the
fundamental decencies of human life! Disloyalty to human
life itself! A perverse and sniggering celebration of the ultimate evil—the evil which rejects not only good but the
possibility of good! Which despises not only charity and
love but the human mind itself with its need of charity; its
necessity of love!

*Mr. Bollingen:* I agree that fascism is precisely such a disloyalty.
And I agree that nothing like Pound's addiction to fascism
—nothing so infantile or so distorted—has accompanied the
perception of the great disorder of our time in other poets.
Baudelaire and Rimbaud and Yeats had their occultism.
Rilke had his self-pity and his fears. But none of them committed the fascist's crime of treason against humanity itself.
Nevertheless the question is not one of the childishness and
perversity of Pound's political beliefs as they are expressed
in this poem. The question is whether their expression here
deprives the poem's insights of their meaning. If it is true

that poetry is an instrument of intuitive knowledge, does it not follow that the presence of opinions in a poem destroys the poem only when the opinions predetermine the intuitions—when they, and not the poet's sensibility, supply the insights? . . . But it is possible, as Dante proves, for the most dogmatic opinions—opinions hateful to multitudes of human beings—to live in a poem beside the most profound and enduring insights, where the poet's overriding loyalty is to his poet's perception of the world. With Pound, as this poem itself demonstrates and as the earlier Cantos make abundantly clear, the loyalty is not to dogmas of fascism but to the poet's vision of a tragic disorder which lies far deeper in our lives and in our time.

*Mr. Saturday:* And yet the dogma does involve the poet. Granted that the vision of disorder is the central preoccupation . . . the fact that Pound himself was attracted to fascism, to put it no more forcefully than that, is relevant to a judgment of the poem. . . . The poet asks you, in effect, to take on faith intuitive perceptions which cannot be tested by reason. How can you take his insights on faith if he discloses himself to you, in the very act of his art, as an adolescent or a crank or a fool who would not recognize man's true experience if it stared him in the face?

*Mr. Bollingen:* But do the poet's opinions so disclose him except when it is *they,* not *he,* that speak to you? Except, that is to say, when the poet is a partisan of opinion who serves his opinions, not his art? . . . You remember Whitehead saying of ancient poets that while their systematic thought "is now nearly worthless . . . their detached insights are priceless."

*Mr. Saturday:* And you think this poem of Pound's has insights such as theirs—this poem written on a dunghill?

*Mr. Bollingen:* Even from the elevation of a dunghill it is possible to see the figure of a man against the stars which is ourselves and which our reason and our science cannot see.

*Mr. Saturday:* And to you it is enough that Pound should see that figure?

*Mr. Bollingen:* And that he made the object which embodies what he saw—the poem. Enough, at least, to justify the judges in their action. . . . I think the poem, with all its evil and its ignorance about it, accomplishes in some measure what a poem should accomplish. I think it accomplishes this because its poet, for all the childishness of his opinions, is loyal in the end not to his opinions but his art.

*Mr. Saturday:* So that the upshot of the whole matter is that Pound's poem is good in spite of its evil. . . .

*Mr. Bollingen:* Not in spite of its evil: including its evil. It is only with its evil about it that this poem can give this poet's vision of his hell. For he himself is damned in it and speaks.

*Mr. Saturday:* So that the upshot of the whole matter is this: that we are to regard the judges in this case as justified because our time expects so little of the art they judged!

*Mr. Bollingen:* Is it so little to ask of any art, even the greatest, that it give mankind, in such an age as ours, an image of our lives?

# Pure Poetry, Impure Politics, and Ezra Pound

## The Bollingen Prize Controversy Revisited

by PETER VIERECK

Not even Ezra Pound's most intolerant belittlers have ever been able to deny his trail-blazing function, whether or not one likes his trails. Therefore one wonders what his feelings must be at watching his pious, humorless disciples—for example, in the recent symposium *An Examination of Ezra Pound*—turn his rebellious originality into a frozen image as stereotyped as that of the Georgians and late-Victorians whom he overthrew. The contrast between his vitality in the 1920's and the stuffiness of his 1950 praetorian guard is brought out by reading his vivid collected *Letters,* also recently published, side by side with *An Examination.* The former book is alive. Much of the latter book is dead with precisely that kind of pompous, pretentious, deadly deadness that Pound was overthrowing in 1913.

The appearance of these two new contrasting books has reopened the dormant Pound controversy of 1949. Both friends and foes of his Bollingen prize award will find effective new ammunition in the symposium. You can prove Pound's disciples to be pure aesthetes or anti-Semitic fascist sympathizers, depending on which particular essays you pick from the book. If you pick Edith Sitwell's chapter, for example, you will find a brilliant appreciation of Pound's artistic techniques, the kind of appreciation that—basing itself on the noble if unreal assumption that art is radically distinct from life—motivated the original Bollingen award. However, not all the contributions are of the same order as Edith Sitwell's. If you turn to certain of the others (perhaps closest to Pound's own intention), you find Pound's fascism and anti-Semitism accepted as inseparable from his poetry. Reading these disciples, one is forced to wonder to what extent his racist "anti-usury" gospels are catching on among the more "advanced" English students and the avant-garde. As Robert Gorham Davis has noted ironically in a review of the book: "After the long religio-critical hiatus of the forties, it is now proper, as in the thirties, to tie up literature with political reform. But what reform it is! . . . Pound is made the master again, and Eliot the shrewd and talented disciple. Money Reform and Fascism become more fashionably topical than Original Sin and Anglicanism."

From the *Examination* symposium, let us cite a few examples of this new topicality. John Drummond finds "cogent reasons for Pound's admiration of Fascism" and coyly suggests that Italy's lack of new ideas "almost forces one to maintain that Fascism's greatest crime was not that it was too hard on the Italians but that it was not hard enough." Max Wykes-Joyce sees Pound's message on fascism and usury as an essential part and purpose of his *Cantos,* and declares: "Fascism carried the implication of something positive. . . . It was based on the progressive prosperity of the whole people; it typified for the many honest Fascists what Pound calls 'the increment of association,' that economic element possible only in a group of people working towards a common end: thus 'the increment of association . . . is affirmed in every fascio clamped to a public building.' . . . His detestation of universal usury accounts for his anti-Semitism. His is economic anti-Semitism. That he is not racially anti-Jewish can be abundantly proved. . . . Among the usurers, however, there are so many Jews; and against that sort of Jew Pound is justly merciless."

"Merciless" is a strong word. Does the "just" kind of mercilessness include the torture and gassing and burning alive of millions? Pound himself evidently thought so when on the Rome radio he approved of the Nazi extermination of Jews.

In the same symposium, Henry Swabey is another who puts first

stress on Pound's supposed political wisdom. Swabey denies that
Pound was "an advocate of despotism" and then quotes without
demur a panegyric of Mussolini's movement by the Fascist propa-
gandist Signora Agresti. Both Wykes-Joyce and Swabey gloss over
Pound's racism by asserting that—some of his best friends were
Jews! Swabey adds such *non sequiturs* as that Pound "is far less
consciously 'racial' in outlook" than was the Jewish statesman
Disraeli. He enthusiastically cites the isolationist attacks of the
Roosevelt-haters on Roosevelt's "aggressive" foreign policy, and
on the "distasteful facts about Pearl Harbor," in order to prove a
fact that is unfortunately all too true: "Pound is not the solitary
crotchet that the mesmeric press would have us believe and was
certainly not alone among Americans in deploring Roosevelt's
policies." With a prim contempt for this decadent democracy of
alleged rackets and racketeers, Swabey concludes that ideologically
"Pound is a genial, if exacting, guide and, although vilification of
him and his work is the latest 'racket' in America, one who has
studied his work cannot quit the subject without a word of gratitude."

There is also Peter Russell, earnest and sincere editor of *An
Examination,* founder of the Ezra Pound Society of London, who
has arranged for publication in England of some of Pound's pro-
Axis and allegedly treasonable broadcasts from Radio Rome. He
says gleefully of the *Cantos* what the anti-Poundians dolefully have
been maintaining all along: "To try to separate the poetic essence
from the didactic substance of the poem would be valueless ped-
antry or, at best, adolescent romantic aestheticism."

It is not intended to suggest by these above quotations that a
purely literary appreciation of Pound is impossible. It goes without
saying that the valuable firm of New Directions—which published
the *Examination*—and its able editor, James Laughlin, have no
use whatever for fascism or racism. Moreover, in this same *Examination,* Hugh Porteus, Hugh Kenner, G. S. Fraser, and others
offer fascinating and mainly literary insights. Only a witch-hunt
mentality could accuse them of sharing the views of Russell, Swabey, Wykes-Joyce, etc., merely because they all appear in the same
book. Examples of both types of Poundians can be multiplied *ad*

*infinitum* if we begin citing the Little Magazines. The fairest thing is to recall that the world contains both Gentle Poundians (the pure aesthetes) and Tough Poundians (those who find in his "just mercilessness" to Jews and usurers a "genial guide"). And both can validly quote scripture (the Book of Ezra?) to their purpose.

Similarly, to draw a strikingly relevant parallel, there were Gentle Wagnerians (those who loved Wagner as a pure musician) and those Tough Wagnerians who preached his proto-Nazism and anti-Semitism and who included Houston Stewart Chamberlain and Adolf Hitler. In Wagner's day those who, like Nietzsche, prophetically feared Wagner's political influence were ridiculed: how could a "crank artist" ever be a political "danger"? Yet in the century that followed, Wagner's metapolitical credo became the main fountainhead of Hitler's ideology.* The prior example of Wagner is perhaps an answer to the Gentle Poundians, who sincerely detest Pound's fascism but deem it no future menace in America. They are ignoring the current resurgence—slight but potentially dangerous—of semi-fascist isolationist rabble-rousers in our yellow press, who ominously treat fascism as the opposite of Stalinism instead of its twin.

On the other hand, much of the moralizing hue and cry against Pound's fascism and Jew-baiting comes not from sincere antifascists but from the envy with which the dwarfs of mediocrity forever regard originality and experimentalism in art. Without telepathy and an impossibly subtle lie-detector machine, we cannot estimate exactly how much of the anti-Pound hue and cry can thus be explained, but certainly a high percentage is involved.

Such is the company one inevitably gets oneself into. Philistia, for example, would exploit my own objections to Pound's receiving the Bollingen prize in a fashion never intended by me: namely, as a demagogic weapon against everything original and novel in poetry, everything that challenges the reader to effort. Yet this playing into wrong hands, though admittedly a danger, is not an ineluctable danger. It all depends on how the matter is handled (just as, for example, anti-Communism can or cannot play into reactionary hands, depending on how it is handled). To illustrate

---

* For detailed documentation of this hypothesis, see my book *Metapolitics: From the Romantics to Hitler* (Knopf, 1941).

this by taking the example nearest home: I am becoming impatient to the point of brusqueness when told that my criticism of certain critics and poets is "unconsciously serving the philistines." The charge would be true if I criticized Pound or the epigones of Eliot in order to praise Edgar Guest or at best Austin Dobson. But the charge becomes a mere diversionary maneuver when I criticize the stifling Pound-Eliot cult in order to praise the more sensuous lyricism of such poets as Yeats, Hart Crane, Theodore Roethke, Richard Wilbur, and Louis Simpson.

The position of really serious, *non*-philistine opponents of the Bollingen prize gets so misrepresented in most periodicals that the following must be stressed (though it ought not to be necessary to stress it): most of us were never impugning the committee's motives or indicting all modern poetry. For us the issue is whether, as some "new critics" believe, form and technique can be considered apart from content and meaning. The sympathies of the committee were not with Pound's politics. Judging by their much debated press release, their sympathies were with the widely held belief—a belief I consider unhistorical and psychologically false but not at all "fascist"—that artistic form can be considered apart from its content and moral meaning.

But it should have been clear that the *Pisan Cantos* were far from being a non-political ivory tower of pure aesthetic formalism. On the contrary, fascism and anti-Semitism compose one of the essential "myths" of these and the earlier *Cantos*. Both earlier and later *Cantos*—and no question of insanity arises with the earlier ones*—proclaim that same fascism and racism which Pound preached over Mussolini's radio.

In *Partisan Review,* May 1949, George Orwell wrote of Pound and his broadcasts: "Some time ago I saw it stated in an American periodical that Pound only broadcast on the Rome radio when 'the balance of his mind was upset.' . . . This is plain falsehood. Pound was an ardent follower of Mussolini as far back as the 1920's and never concealed it. He was a contributor to Mosley's review, the *British Union Quarterly*. . . . His broadcasts were disgusting.

---

* Pound's treason trial was suspended on a ruling of insanity, a ruling challenged as incorrect by the psychiatrist Frederic Wertham.

I remember at least one in which he approved the massacre of the East European Jews and 'warned' the American Jews that their turn was coming presently. . . . He *may* be a good writer (I must admit that I personally have always regarded him as an entirely spurious writer), but the opinions that he has tried to disseminate [in] his works are evil. . . ."

Obviously, Pound has a right to publish anything whatever, with any opinions whatever. But should he also get a prize for it? Perhaps yes, if it were for his distinguished literary career as a whole. Unfortunately, the Bollingen prize was solely for one book: *The Pisan Cantos;* and while poems of aesthetic intention must be judged aesthetically, regardless of their author's politics, Pound's prize-winning poem was not intended as purely aesthetic. Its message politically was that Mussolini was martyred and World War II caused by Jews: "the goyim go to saleable slaughter" for "the yidd," known as "David rex the prime s.o.b." This is politics, not serious poetry, hence not exempt from ethical, as well as aesthetic, condemnation.

Whether from a famous coterie-protected poet, or from a mere "low-brow" Gerald L. K. Smith, such racist propaganda must be protested by those to whom a single human compassion for Hitler's millions of tortured victims is the deepest emotional and moral experience of our era. What, indeed, is our urgently necessary zeal against Communism but this same heart-breaking distress over inhumanity? To fellow authors who indiscriminately blacken the motives of all critics of *The Pisan Cantos,* we repeat Cromwell's plea, in humility and in sincere good will: "Think it possible that you may be mistaken." Is it anti-poetic and philistine to feel rather violently about *The Pisan Cantos* and other influential neo-fascist revivals when one hears of an ex-Nazi official boasting this year in Frankfort that, when Jewish mothers asked him where their missing two-year-old babies went, he replied: "Up the chimney!"

Message aside, there is much downright bad writing in the *Pisan Cantos.* William Barrett wisely asked in *Partisan Review:* "How far is it possible, in a lyric poem, for technical embellishments to transform vicious and ugly matter into beautiful poetry?" But really, now, would even the proverbially objective observer from Mars, utterly free from anti-fascist "prejudices," be able to find any "technical embellishments" or "beautiful poetry" in the following lines from the *Pisan Cantos:* "Pétain defended Verdun while Blum was defending a bidet"; "Geneva the usurers' dunghill/Frogs, brits, with a few dutch pimps."

Nevertheless, the bad writing of most of this book is a point I raise only in passing and one I am unwilling, though not unable, to stress. Stressing it would reduce the argument of this article to too easy a plane. If the book (as I believe) is badly written, then even the advocates of art for art's sake would oppose its award. The problem is made more difficult for those who opposed the award— more difficult but also more important and basic—if we temporarily pretend "for the sake of the argument" that it *is* well written and then add: *even in that case* we would oppose the award. Not on political grounds. Poetry must never be judged by politics. But on grounds that our entire civilization, including poetry, depends almost completely on our constantly maintaining a moral heritage which Nazi anti-Semitism would destroy.

Anti-fascist admirers of Pound, writing in honest bewilderment, have asked me personally why Pound's fascism, though admittedly evil, should spoil his poetry for me when the anti-democratic views and alleged "bad politics" of Dante or Shakespeare obviously do not spoil their poetry for me in the slightest. The answer is that Nazi anti-Semitism is not, except ephemerally and superficially, politics at all but a uniquely obscene anti-ethics, a metaphysics of satanism. There is no such metaphysics, no such ethical obscenity basic to Dante or Shakespeare; one may disagree with their monarchism, but this disagreement does not affect the value of their poetry: no basic challenge to civilization is involved in it.

A seemingly more telling argument on the part of the defenders of the Bollingen prize is to recite the familiar list of the great and admittedly moral authors of the past who happened to dislike Jews. But is it really fair, in defense of Pound and of his award, to cite the anti-Semitism and anti-usury of Shakespeare's *Merchant of Venice?* One contributor to *An Examination of Ezra Pound* does so almost gloatingly, and indeed, the Nazis during the war performed the *Merchant of Venice* with glee. Does this analogy undermine

Shakespeare in our regard or bolster Pound? Or is it false and misleading?

Probably false and misleading. Though racial prejudice is never a good thing, the extent to which it is a bad thing varies tremendously according to the age and the moral and social context. Though abstractly just as wrong in Shakespeare's day as now, anti-Semitism was then not in such blunt defiance of the limited information available to that age; nor was it the spearhead of a sinister assault on liberty itself; nor was there a background of sadistic mass murder even remotely approaching Belsen and Ravensbrueck. Today we "know better" (or at least ought to, from the psychological and historical information generally available). It was infinitely more difficult for an Elizabethan to "know better" about anti-Semitism than for Pound. Anti-Semitism in Shakespeare's day was to some extent a norm, even for men of good intentions, while today it represents the very worst and most ill-intentioned forces of our age.

Moreover, Shakespeare gives dignity to, and arouses his readers' sympathy for, the predicament of Shylock. There is a world of difference artistically and also ethically between Shakespeare's letting Shylock express the common humanity of: "I am a Jew. If you prick us, do we not bleed?" and Pound's joking reference to mass murder as "fresh meat on the Russian steppes," the most callous single reference ever written by an American artist.

Pre-Belsen and post-Belsen anti-Semitism, though both unjustified, are qualitatively different; and the former (Shakespeare or Voltaire) cannot be logically compared to the latter (Pound or Céline).* The burning or gassing of five or six million Jews gave, from that point on, an entirely new dimension to anti-Semitism. Anti-Semitism after Belsen becomes a uniquely loathsome insult to all Christian ideals, to all human aspirations, to the very core of the dignity of man. This was not the case with the pre-Nazi anti-Semitism of a Shakespeare, a Voltaire, or a Henry Adams. Wrong? Yes. Beyond the pale? Hardly.

---

* Here I am oversimplifying for brevity's sake. Naturally, there were pogroms during the Crusades, the Inquisition, and in czarist Russia. But they did not involve, morally and personally, a Shakespeare or a Voltaire, as closely as Belsen does the Axis broadcaster, Pound; and there are further obvious distinctions (such as religious persecution versus racial persecution) making Nazi genocide *sui generis*.

Even if, for the sake of the broader issue, we concede the fantastic hypothesis that the *Pisan Cantos* are great poetry, in that case— while respecting such greatness and defending its right of free speech—we must still raise the issue of whether this in addition requires the public honor of an award. Either fascist anti-Semitism is "beyond the bounds of our intellectual life" (to quote the following comment from Irving Howe), or it isn't: "To give Pound a literary prize is, willy-nilly, a moral act within the frame of our social world. To honor him is to regard him as a man with whom one can have decent, normal, even affectionately respectful human and intellectual relations; it means to extend a hand of public fraternity to Ezra Pound. Now a hand to help him when he is down, yes. A hand to defend him from censors, fools and blood-seekers, yes. But a hand of honor and congratulations, no. For Pound, by virtue of his public record and utterances, is beyond the bounds of our intellectual life. If the judges felt that he had written the best poetry of 1948, I think they should have publicly said so—but not awarded any prize for the year."

How is it that no truly elegant avant-garde critic, when praising Pound, deigns to express qualms about: (1) the immoral political message or (2) the unintelligibility of the non-political parts of the poem? This irresponsible qualmlessness about immorality and about unclarity would seem to be the result of two prevalent attitudes, originally liberating but now exerting a despotism of their own. The two attitudes are: first, the triumph of detailed textual criticism for its own sake, scorning the "heresy of paraphrasing" a poem's meaning and ethical content; second, the pushing of T. S. Eliot's plausible statement that modern poetry must be complex into an anxiety neurosis where critics are scared of ever objecting to obscurity lest they sound like middle-brows instead of like Sensitive Plants.

The famous New Criticism's method of analysis tends to treat a poem by itself, like a self-created airtight-sealed object, outside cause and effect. By discarding a poem's *irrelevant* historical, psychological, and "moralizing" encrustations, the "new critics" have splendidly taught us to read the text itself. But by also discarding the *relevant* historical, psychological, and ethical aspects, they are often misreading the text itself.

A reader's response to a poem is a total response, a *Gestalt* in which aesthetic as well as ethical, psychological, and historical factors are inseparably fused together. It is a self-deception to try to separate them and to discover some alchemistical quintessence of isolated "pure" aesthetics, to be judged only by certified "pure" mandarins of criticism. It may be argued that this inextricability of form and content is undesirable; in any case, that it exists is undeniable, with the *Pisan Cantos* only one example among many. This inextricability prompted Paul Valéry's wise warning: "To construct a poem that contains only poetry is impossible. If a piece contains only poetry, it is not constructed; it is not a poem."

So independent an observer as Harry Levin has summarized some of the pros and cons as follows: "Spingarn had called for 'the new criticism' in 1910, without receiving very much response. John Crowe Ransom called again in 1941—and this time spirits came from the vasty deep. It is salutary that criticism, which is bound to admit a good deal of extraneous matter, should thus renew itself for each generation by returning to the direct contemplation of the artistic object. The danger is that the critic who limits his purview too narrowly, is apt to misinterpret the text upon which he dwells. Critics of the new critics, however, have adduced enough specific reminders that interpretation of the present requires acquaintance with the past. . . . We may well be faced, when the situation crystallizes, with a new academicism. The issue will then be whether it is more enlightening, less occult than the old." (Preface to *Perspectives of Criticism.*)

To Archibald MacLeish's splendid statement about poetry ("a poem should not mean but be") must be added the belief that a poem should both mean and be. Only to be, leads to hermetic "new critic" formalism. Only to mean, leads to demagogy, the wrong kind of popularity, and ultimately to the fatal exploitation of literature by Agitprop, which is not really "democratic," as claimed, but either commercial (in America) or totalitarian (in Soviet and fellow-traveler circles).

The current battle of "obscurity" versus "clarity" (or of "to be" versus "to mean") tends to divide poets into two extremes equally deadly to poetry. The first extreme, in the name of anti-philistinism, is for crossword-puzzle poetry which, whatever its fascination, would kill poetry by scaring away its audience. The second extreme, in the name of communication, would demagogically popularize poetry, in betrayal of all integrity of standards, until it reaches the widest but also lowest common denominator and is no longer poetry at all, but verse. The first group would sterilize the muse. The second group would prostitute her.

Is there no third possibility for the serious craftsman? Must he become either *précieux* or "corny," either Babbitt Junior or Babbitt Senior?

The answer is: an act of creative faith in a new and third force in poetry, already emerging, equally remote from the muse's mincing sterilizers and back-slapping salesmen. Such a third force must prefer a difficult simplicity to an easy obscurity. It must return to the function of ethical responsibility and of communication of ideas and emotions. Any fool can lucidly communicate an easy greeting-card level of ideas and emotions. Any fool can obscurely "impress" a would-be modernist reader by incoherent and pretentious approximations of difficult ideas and emotions. Great art communicates lucidly and with classic simplicity the most difficult level of ideas and emotions.

It is not easy to say how the new young poets of the mid-century can ever achieve the vitality and originality of the Eliot and Pound movement of three decades ago. But it is easy to say how they can never achieve it: namely, by continuing to imitate Eliot and Pound, whose great virtue—which atones for great harm—is that they were not imitators. "Woe to you," said Goethe, "if you are a grandson!" Pound's and Eliot's ubiquitous "grandsons" have turned the antiphilistinism of their masters into a snobbish new philistinism. Marx said: *"Je ne suis pas Marxiste."* Freud, fortunately, was no Freudian. The time has come for Eliot to ask: "Who will protect me from my protégés?"

These devout grandsons have played Pound a worse trick than anything intended by those of us who cannot enjoy his *Cantos*. They have frozen his dynamic experimental zest, which three decades ago was still doing more good than harm, into a static Alexandrian school. Disarmingly, really endearingly humorous, their school would do no harm even today, were it not for the well-meaning tyranny of its literary Party Line (now beginning to crumble) over college English departments and Little Magazines.

Pound is the keystone of this school of criticism; if he goes out of fashion, then the whole structure becomes shaky; hence, the violence of the attacks on the "philistinism" of critics of the Bollingen prize. These attacks (in some instances, it should be repeated, quite justified) are for the most part motivated not by sympathy with the Master's politics but either by an honorable appreciation of Pound's genius or else by the strategy of sectarian literary patronage systems. Can we distinguish which is which? "For reasons of personal loyalty, which one must respect, and for reasons of sectarian literary loyalty, which one may or may not respect," wrote Karl Shapiro of the Bollingen prize, "few poets anywhere are in a position to say what they really think of Pound's work." In either case, our Allen Tate—to name one brilliant and typical pupil of the Pound-Eliot school—have Alexandrianized and Babbittized this work, *not* into a "fascist" conspiracy, as some *Saturday Review of Literature* writers absurdly implied, but into a supreme bore. They have turned the vital and original revolt of 1913 and the 1920's into a New Academy, today's most baneful block to vitality and originality.

In overcoming this road block, the growing revolt may be rejuvenating poetry as once the Eliot-Pound revolt did in its first exciting dawn. The American poetry of the future, like the classicism of the ancient past, will again see art as a groping search for the good, the true, the beautiful; all three as potentially harmonizing rather than conflicting. What if you seek only the beautiful? Suppose, like so much "new" criticism, you passively ignore the good and the true? Or suppose, like the fascist diabolism of some of Pound's *Cantos,* you actively attack the good and the true? In such cases, you usually find yourself losing the beautiful also. You will find the beautiful only when you seek more than the beautiful.

# Weekend with Ezra Pound

by DAVID RATTRAY

It was raining in Washington when I arrived, and the dull red building of St. Elizabeth's seemed particularly discouraging. After checking in at the main office, I climbed the spiral stairs, all steel and dirty enamel, chipped and peeling walls, to the heavy black door of Ezra Pound's ward, and rang the bell. I could hear radio music inside.

A Negro attendant with a great jingling ring of keys let me in. Half a dozen patients gathered round a TV set next to the door. The hall was very wide and dark as a subway station. There were benches on either side, and patients were sitting or lying on them. Doors opened on rooms for two or three, and there were several alcoves where rooms might have been, with tables for games, and chairs. Pound and his wife, with a young novelist named Jean Marie Châtel, and a painter, Miss Martinelli, were sitting in one of these alcoves when I arrived.

Pound sprang up from the canvas lawn-chair and shook my hand. "You're Rattray? How fortunate you got here at this moment—John here was just beginning to be tiresome, and so now," and he laid his hand on the chair in which Châtel was still sitting, next to his own, "*he* will sit over there, and you may sit here." Châtel, looking a little embarrassed, took a seat in the corner on the other side of the round game table. Pound picked up his overcoat from the arm of my chair and flung it across the table after him.

He sat back down, in a reclining position with his legs crossed, eyes half closed, looking exactly as he did in the Wyndham Lewis portrait made many years ago. His hair is now white all over and he is getting bald. He was dressed in tan shorts too big for him, tennis shoes and a loose plaid shirt. His face looks weathered, like that of a man who has worked outdoors all his life. His heavy-wristed hands are coarse and calloused, but the fingernails neatly cut short and square. I was surprised by the appearance of his arms and legs. There was no sign of that flabbiness that comes even to some of the strongest men in their forties and fifties. The Greeks spoke of "old age that unstrings men's knees," but as I watched Pound stride up and down, his knees strung taut, his calves bulging like an athlete's, I thought of some lines from Ramon Guthrie's poem, "E. P. in Paris and Elsewhere":

> "This is not walking.
> This is stalking, pacing
> as done by jaguar or ounce
> in Zagreus' days, tracing
> the lay-out for the Labyrinth . . ."

Before we had a chance to talk about anything, Pound jumped up again: "You'll have tea, won't you?"

I said that I would, and immediately he was everywhere at once, in a frenzy of activity, loading himself with jars of various sizes, tin boxes of sugar and tea, spoons and a saucer. I stood up in embarrassment, not knowing what I ought to do, but Mrs. Pound beckoned me from her corner: "Let's sit here and talk while he makes the tea." She was sitting behind a ramshackle old upright piano, so as not to see the people in the hall or be seen by them. Miss Martinelli was making sketches for a portrait of her.

Suddenly Pound was standing before me, holding out a peanut butter jar filled with hot tea. When we got settled again, he glared up at me and said, "Well, what specific questions have you? Or did you just come to talk? I'd just as soon talk."

So we talked quietly. Pound took a sip of his tea and sat back with his eyes closed. I sipped nervously at mine. Miss Martinelli went on sketching Mrs. Pound, the two seated next to the barred windows, in which the gray day peered uncertainly, through a tangle of wet vines laced over the trellis-work of the bars. It was dark in the alcove, but a bare electric bulb blazed from the high ceiling of the hall. Châtel, with his back to it, was reading, his face concealed from us by a huge newspaper, *Truth*. I hitched my chair over out of the light.

"D. P. has a beautiful face," said Miss Martinelli, "I think she has a beautiful profile, but it is so *difficult* . . . yes, of course, that's why. Maestro . . ."

"Yes Ma'am," said Pound, jerking around to sit on the edge of his chair.

"Will you look at this drawing?" Pound looked at it, squinting in the light, then said, "It's a likeness," and swung himself violently back into the reclining position.

I told him I was planning to spend a few weeks in Dalmatia.

"So you're going to the Damnation Coast? Don't know what the Hell you'll see there, do you?" I said that I had friends in Split and Dubrovnik. One of them was a painter, who wanted to show me the medieval frescoes.

"If I were you, then, I should get to the heart of the matter, and see them in Turkey. I hear they've done a lot of work there recently, restoring them where the Turks had painted 'em over." He told me about a Professor Pearson of Yale, who is an adviser on the selection of Square Dollar Books ("American textbooks for students who want first things first") and who is very interested in Byzantine frescoes. He jumped up and rushed to his room to type Pearson's address.

"You could make an appointment with him if you happen to be passing through there any time. He'd confirm what I told you about medieval Greek. Now there's something that's wide open, plenty there's not even published yet, not chewed and hashed. . . . Now you're talking to an old man that never learned his Greek properly, but you, you're lucky, to know it at the beginning of the game. But I know it well enough to recognize style when I see it, and Psellus' style, he's seventh or eighth century, Psellus in the Chronographia, he writes with the precision and economy of Flaubert or the Goncourts. And Psellus had enough perception to see 'em fall into just about the same categories they do today. He knows the difference between true credit and *creatio ex nihil*. . . . So you're

going to southern France next year. Well, I've been trying to make
some people wake up to a number of simple facts, and they'd better
hurry up, if they don't want to wake up too late to *do* anything.
Now if you want to *do* some really live historical research, something that hasn't been chewed over, look into Bertran, Bertran de
Born I mean, '*Baros mettez en gatge* . . .' you know the one I
mean, 'Barons, hock your castles.' You'll probably walk that country a lot, and see those castles, the ones he was talking about, the
ones they *hocked*. Bertran knew a usurer when he saw one—they
hocked 'em to go on crusade, you know. That would be some *useful* research, what you told your reader, your reader could put to
use—the area still suffers from when they put their lands *en gatge*
—you could find out for yourself, and tell your reader what happens when you hock your castles to the Jews."

Mrs. Pound interrupted this tirade by telling about the walks
they took together in southern France.

"We always used Toulouse as our base. Toulouse itself is a
mediocre town, but one comes to grow fond of it, and the country
all around is as beautiful and full of Provence as any place else in
the South. I went with him on his last two walks. We had been
married only a short time, and we went all over with rucksacks,
and slept outdoors, but then the War interrupted all that."

"I don't suppose," said Pound, "that the old cupboard is still
there, the one that was bulging with pornographic books. And old
Pere—is dead. Now let me see who *is* still alive." Then he slowly
unraveled the number of his acquaintances now living in France,
who were interested in Provençal literature: Laubies, Vanderply,
Pellizzi ('a civilized wop') and Brancusi ('probably gaga by now,
if alive at all'), and told an anecdote about each.

"And you *could* go see old Aldington as to Greek or Provençal,
but better not as from E. P.; you'd better just be the *jeune homme
modeste*. He lives in Montpellier now, I believe."

Mrs. Pound repeated the list of poets and scholars back to him,
counting them off on her fingers, and he went to his room and
typed their names and addresses for me.

When he came back, we sat for a while in silence. It was late
afternoon. Miss Martinelli was perched like a bird at dusk, her

feet planted on the rung of the wooden chair. She was still at work on her sketch. Looking at her, with her golden hair falling down around her thin shoulders, I thought of Pound's line,

In the gloom the gold gathers the light against it.

She was dressed in blue jeans and a checkered blouse. Her appearance suggested a frayed and faded survivor of the early bobby-sox days. She had huge eyes like a cat. They bulged in a flushed face that tapered down from an enormous forehead to a tiny chin and tinier double chin. Her lips were tight and pale, but sometimes relaxed and parted into a naive smile. I assumed that she was a patient from another ward.

Pound jumped up and strode across the hall to his room, making a sign for me to follow him. He gave me one of the Square Dollar books, *Roman and Moslem Moneys* by Alexander Del Mar. The notice on the jacket informed me that Del Mar was among those "American writers who can hold their own, either as stylists or historians, against any foreign competition whatsoever," who are being printed by the Square Dollar Series. I was further impressed by the following paragraph on the opposite cover:

> The sheer incompetence, triviality and worthlessness of our universities is nowhere more blatantly exposed than in their ignorance of Del Mar's writings, published from 1862 onwards in both London and the U.S. Had one not met some of the low-grade personnel of the faculties, one would be unable to attribute the historical blackout to anything save the great conspiracy which some fanatics claim to be at the root of it.

Pound's room was strewn with wadded papers, bits of envelopes, trampled books, pencils, lengths of string, cardboard files, trunks, old paint cans, jars filled with teabags or scraps of food. The walls were hung with paintings, some by Miss Martinelli. There was a dressing table with a huge mirror which reflected the glow of sunset, and filled the room with it. The old man dove under the table looking for a couple of large tin paint cans. I noticed again how strong his bare legs looked. A person who saw him that afternoon might have had the impression, not of a poet who had lived ten years in the sordid prison described by MacLeish, but of an old-time seaman, aged but still spry from climbing the rigging every day, sitting at his ease in a coffee-house or tavern between voyages of exploration or privateering on the Spanish Main. He pulled out the tins and pried them open. They were filled with doughnuts and bread. He put some into a paper bag and tossed it to Miss Martinelli, who was standing at the door. Then he poked around under the bed until he found a box filled with boiled eggs and salami. This he handed to me to give to Châtel. It was marked *Books,* sent by Witter Bynner.

When we reached the big black door at the other end of the hall, near the TV set, Miss Martinelli saw a pair of singing comedians on the screen,

"Look at those fairies! Isn't it disgusting?"

Pound threw his arms around her, hugged her, and kissed her goodbye. He turned and asked me to come the next day. The attendant unlocked the door while we made our farewells. I was a little surprised to see that Châtel and Miss Martinelli were only visitors.

Châtel put me up for the night on a couch. We had the food Pound had given him for supper, and talked about literature and politics for several hours. He told me that he and Miss Martinelli were supplied with almost all their food by Pound, who gets it from the hospital cafeteria. In our conversation he revealed himself as a fanatic disciple of the "Maestro"; he apes his every like and dislike, even imitates his nervous tics and manner of speaking, and way of jumping up and stalking around. Next morning his father invited us to lunch.

Châtel's father, now a modest insurance man, was before the war a *colon* in Algeria; then joined the Free French and emigrated after the war. While we were at lunch, Châtel showed his father the copy of *Truth* which Pound had lent him, and which was filled with financiers, munitions manufacturers, a McFadden speech of 1932, and a "recently uncovered" Rothschild letter of 1862, "when America was sold to the Jews." M. Châtel read page after page, murmuring *"Très intéressant, très intéressant. . . ."*

While we were on the way from his father's to St. Elizabeth's, I asked my young companion if there might be some connection between the Kasper of Kasper & Horton Square Dollar Books, and the Kasper of Clinton, Tennessee. He laughed loudly and slapped his gloved hand on the steering wheel: "Ah! at last, the Great Dawning . . . why yes, of course, they're one and the same."

Kasper had recently opened a bookshop in Georgetown, D.C., organized the Seaboard White Citizens' Council and affiliated it to similar councils in the Deep South.

The group aimed to end "integration" in Washington, put the NAACP on the Attorney General's "subversive list" and abolish "rock-and-roll." Membership was open to anyone 18 and white, who "believes in the divinity of Jesus Christ." Jews were not allowed. *The New York Times* quotes from a pamphlet sent out by the Council. It condemns "pink punks . . . freaks, golf players, poodle dogs, hot-eyed Socialists, Fabians, scum, mold on top of the omelette . . . liars for hire, the press gang, degenerate liberals crying for the petrefaction of putrefaction."

The phrase "petrefaction of putrefaction" had rung a familiar note, and I must have suspected what Châtel's answer would be, but it wasn't till then that my mind began to work, and the passage quoted above came to me, together with Cantos XIV and XV, Pound's Inferno, and the following phrases from them:

> n and the press gang
> And those who had lied for hire . . .
> . . . a circle of lady golfers . . .
> and the fabians crying for the petre-
> faction of putrefaction . . .

I mentioned this to Châtel. The sun had just broken through the clouds and was kindling a fire in his stiff brown bush of hair, lighting up his pale unshaven face, marred by pimples and a huge insect bite on the forehead, while his coarse features labored with excitement.

"Of course, of course," he said with a wave of his hand, and stepped on the gas. "And you know what else was in that proclamation . . . no, you could never guess, because the book he took it from was burned up by order of the International Jews after the war, every copy they could lay hands on. The important part, where he sets forth the economic program, is straight from Feder . . . Gottfried Feder, do you know who he was?"

I indicated by a smiling nod and a properly righteous shudder that I did.

"Feder's book on the Nazi Economics. That's the important thing, the Negro business is just a front, he knows it's the only way he can get the Southern farmers to vote for him, but *then,* when he gets the power (and they've already won here and there, Charlottesville is one place) then, he can get to work on the economic program."

I wondered, as we turned up the road to St. Elizabeth's, if Pound might not have turned out that "Seaboard" pamphlet, and had a hand in *Truth* as well. As it happened, I came away convinced of it, having met the Maestro in an Economic Mood that afternoon, and also made the acquaintance of Mr. Horton of Kasper & Horton.

When Châtel and I arrived, Mrs. Pound was already sitting in her corner. Pound said:

"Glad you could come again. Hell of a lot better company than what he brought with him yesterday, I'm sure. Sit down and I'll make you some tea."

Mrs. Pound explained that an uninvited caller had made his way into the ward with Châtel, having given him to understand that he was invited by Pound and authorized by the hospital. I asked who he was.

"He is a journalist and we don't like him. In fact, E. P. has a violent aversion to him, and so we got the attendant and had the man ejected."

I started to question Pound about Provençal music, and he said he had heard that more than 250 tunes survive, but he didn't know where they were published.

"Oh yes, it seems to me that one of those old fellows, the ones I told you about yesterday—could it have been Pellizzi?—one of them told me something about a facsimile edition being printed in Barcelona. Of course you know that most of those old manuscripts are just *motz* without *sons*. I've seen 'em with the staves carefully drawn on, but no *sons*, just the verses underneath, an entirely understandable bit of laziness: the fellow knew how it went, a perfectly simple tune, why waste time writing it all out? And as you know, transcribing those songs from the original to the modern notation is a job for a musicologist. Maybe that's why so few have been published. But you know, that old notation, it's just a kind of musical shorthand, an aid to memory, to be used only by someone who had already heard the tune at least once."

I told him about the record of Provençal songs made by Yves Tessier, who in addition to being a musicologist was an excellent singer. He waved his hand impatiently.

"Don't expect Grandpa to know anything about Provençal after 1920. That's all after my time. You have my *Spirit of Romance?* You do? All right, I cover all that in there."

I had noticed several times before Pound's unwillingness to be told anything that he hadn't already found out for himself; and yet, he declares that he never reads anything unless it's going to teach him something.

"At my age I can't waste the time. I read for information. I am not on the examination board to determine whether a young fellow's past the sophomore level in writing, or whether he should graduate with senior honors. I used to do it when I was young, but now I leave it to the young men . . . But speaking of notation as an aid to memory, that's the way I did my opera *Villon*. I have the only copy in existence over there in my room. BBC put it on in 1932 and they had some copies, but lost them. Too bad they didn't make a record of it, because I wrote out the *motz el sons* just the way the old troubadours did, just as an aid to memory. I used the modern notation in the old simple shorthand way, and I can read it, but nobody else can without hearing it first—I could hum it or whistle it to 'em. I don't have much of a voice to carry a tune, singing, but whistling or humming, I could make it clear to the musicians. They wanted to do it again, and get the tunes from me here, with a tape recorder. No, that wouldn't be any good, I'd have to rehearse it with 'em the way I did before. Imagine, recording engineers, singers, all swarming around in *here*—it would be a madhouse. . . ."

His eyes were shining with good humor, and we laughed.

"No, that's one project'll have to wait till I get out of pokey. I guess I'll have some more tea; how about you?"

Miss Martinelli appeared just as Pound was gathering up the jars and tins for tea-making. She was wrapped in a heavy wool overcoat and a long winding scarf, and was flushed and winded. Pound embraced her and ran his hands through her hair, and they talked excitedly, each interrupting the other. I turned and talked with Mrs. Pound. Miss Martinelli sat down in her chair and piled her things on the floor, announcing to us that she had been working since five o'clock that morning.

"At this time last Sunday," said Mrs. Pound, "he was making a record of his own readings. An old friend of his from BBC, a man we knew we could trust, brought one of those tape machines. He's never consented to have a record of his reading hawked in the market place, turned out by one of the great American nonsense factories. But he's known this man for years, and we know he's honest."

"What did you read?" I asked him.

"Well, it wasn't anything really serious. I just wanted to get something on record. I conceived the whole thing more or less as a ribbing for Eliot. Eliot is like that old mule, you light a fire under his tail to get him started, and he goes forward just far enough to burn up the wagon. That's neither here nor there. Anyway I read *'l'Homme Moyen Sensuel'* (first time I'd looked at the damned thing for years), the *Usura* Canto, one of the John Adams, a couple of the Alfred Venison poems, and the preface I did for her book."

He made a gesture toward Miss Martinelli.

"I just wanted to give the old boy a jolt, some time when he's settling down for a nice cozy evening, if he turns on the Third Programme and hears E. P. reading Alfred Venison—I chose the ones he likes the least . . . As for her preface, I wanted to give her a boost. She's one of the few American painters of any promise, that I know of. The Esperia people in Milano did a book, in color, of her paintings last year, and I wrote the preface."

A dark hulking man, dressed in a black overcoat, appeared.

"Hello, Dave," said Pound. It was Mr. Horton.

In the gloom of the alcove his wavy hair and clothing were black, but Horton's face shone white, soft and slippery, as if crudely modeled in soap. I grasped his huge, soft hand. His eyes narrowing suspiciously, he smiled, parting lubber lips to reveal a pair of fang-like eyeteeth.

He sat down on the piano stool, opposite Pound and me, and produced a letter from his coat pocket.

"It seems that Wang has lost an important address book.* He's been staying at the Dartmouth Club in N.Y., and says there's a Jew been hanging around his room, hasn't been able to get rid of him. Says he suspects him of stealing the address book. Here, he says, '. . . contains names of all our nationalist friends and those working for our cause . . .' What the Hell do you think he's done with it? He enclosed this example of the Jew's handwriting."

He handed Pound a creased slip of paper with the following words crudely penciled in a large hand: "The home of the Jews is Israel."

Pound held it up to the light. "So this is a specimen of the Hebe's calligraphy. Strange thing for him to be writing."

"And the funny thing," continued Horton, "is that it looked exactly like Kasper's hand to me."

At this comment, I had to hold my mouth just right to keep from laughing.

I had known Wang fairly well while he was at college, and besides finding him personally repellent, I had concluded that he didn't amount to much, as a poet, or anything else. He has become a legend on campus, an object of ridicule for both teachers and students. But I'd never suspected *how* stupid and conceited he was till Pound showed me a letter Wang had written him.

"Remarkably sensitive to the language for a young Chink," said Pound, looking at me sharply and grinning, as he handed me the letter.

I wondered as I read if Pound really meant it, or was just baiting me. In it Wang referred to himself in the third person, as "Hsin"— his Chinese given name for all I know; it means "Heart-mind." His letter was filled with phrases such as "the Cause which alone keeps

---

* David R. Wang, a member of the Dartmouth class of 1955, is distinguished as being the only Chinese poet of record who devotes himself to the cause of white supremacy. Since graduation, *The Dartmouth* reports, Wang has been touring the Ivy League colleges with the purpose of setting up White Citizens' councils on the campuses. He has characterized Secretary of State Dulles as a "wishy-washy Socialist."

body and soul together, in this horrible city where all stinks of
Jewry." The last sentence was "P.S. Hsin has learned, from a re-
liable source, that *Hudson* has been selling E. P.'s typescripts to
the Jews."

"How ridiculous," said Mrs. Pound.

"What difference would it make if they were, because at least
they're publishing them."

"I don't think they would," said Pound, "I know the editor and
he's honest. I think *Hudson* is honest. Now that's the kind of mon-
keyshine I wouldn't put past Laughlin, you know, Laughlin of 'No
Directions.' "

"There are very powerful elements opposed to the publication of
the Cantos, you know," said Châtel.

"It was 'No Directions' that suppressed that passage about the
Rothschilds in *The Pisan Cantos*," said Pound. "They wanted to
leave the whole thing out without any indication of the omission,
and I said, 'Black lines or nothing' and so in went the black lines,
so all my readers could see the censorship. I guess they were afraid
of losing the support of the New York banks, if they published the
truth about international finance."

"And so," said Miss Martinelli, "Grandpa's got to do it with
suicide troops. Like Kasper. Kasper is your suicide troops. I have
a strange feeling about him. I have a feeling that he is going to die
very soon. And Horton is our coming President."

Horton laughed, "No, no, don't say that. That's looking too far
ahead."

"But has one of my prophecies ever failed?" said Miss Martinelli.
"You know perfectly well that every one of them has come true.
Grandpa says I know intuitively what it takes a great genius years of
study to learn."

During the rest of the afternoon Pound and Horton discussed their
mutual political acquaintances. Pound was continually shuffling in
his recent mail, and pulling out letters and pamphlets which he
would hand to Horton. Horton tried to keep up with these, pursing
his lips and murmuring as he scanned each one, before Pound
thrust another at him.

I noticed two Negroes sitting at a game table in a similar alcove just across the hall, both of them dressed in rumpled baggy suits and wearing pushed-in felt hats. They were playing checkers, but each seemed oblivious of the other. Once they pushed the checker board aside and talked loudly a minute in some unintelligible dialect. Then hitching their chairs over, they faced the checker board again. After a long pause, one of them carefully reached out both hands and moved two pieces at once. In a moment both men were moving pieces at random all over the board. When they stopped, one of the Negroes shuffled over to our alcove and stood in front of Pound, staring out the window, and extending an upturned palm. Without hesitation Pound reached into the pockets of his outsized drawers and fished up a handful of small change. With an abstracted air he selected a dime and a nickel and dropped them into the pink palm, then turned back to the stack of papers in his lap. The Negro stood there a moment, then turned without a word or even a glance at Pound, and stuffing the coins into his coat pocket, he went back across the hall. No one else had paid any attention to this little scene.

Pound pulled out a proofsheet of his biography which will appear in the next *Who's Who,* in which he pointed to a sentence vindicating his war-time actions.

"I had a Hell of a time with 'em over that, and told 'em they couldn't print the thing without that sentence, so they put it in."

It was time to leave, and Pound embraced Miss Martinelli as on the day before. As we went down the stairs, she said, "Grandpa loves me. It's because I symbolize the spirit of Love to him, I guess."

"It's true," said Châtel. "He wrote a whole passage in the 'Rock-Drill' about her."

I didn't have a chance to find out where that passage was.

We stood talking in front of Horton's shabby black car. A middle-aged Jewish couple walked down a nearby path, both of them extremely short and fat.

"Just look at those twin spheres!" said Miss Martinelli, giggling delightedly, "Isn't it too disgusting for words!"

Horton pulled a portrait of himself from the back seat of his car. He said his wife had done it, and it was just about her first painting.

"Oh, what a wonderful job for an amateur," said Miss Martinelli, "I can hardly believe it. Just think of it, her first painting."

I have seen portraits of great dictators, the kind that are printed in color and hung on every wall. Whether of Stalin, Hitler or Tito, they seem to run to a type, and his portrait of Horton was a crude imitation of that type. It was Horton conceived as Our Leader, the Square Dollar President. The painter had given him a hearty complexion, removed his double chin, re-modeled his burly chest and shoulders, straightened his nose, lightened his lips, taken the heaviness from his eyelids and contrived to give him a calm and determined gaze.

I was taking leave of Mrs. Pound when the door of the building we'd just left flew open, and there stood Pound on the doorstep, waving a sheaf of paper in his hand.

"Hey John, come back here and take your god-damned manuscript! How the Hell are you going to become a novelist if you leave your work all over the place? Goodbye Dave, you'll come over Christmas Day, won't you?"

He nodded smilingly at us, and disappeared in the door with a little wave.

Châtel and Miss Martinelli gave me a ride to the railroad station.

# The Case of Ezra Pound

by JACK LAZEBNIK

Ezra Pound will probably die at St. Elizabeth's Hospital for the mentally ill in Washington. Arraigned for treason but never brought to trial, called insane (mentally incompetent) although he continues to publish with great critical success, Pound has not been out of the hospital grounds for eleven years now, held "in the long, dim corridor inhabited by the ghosts of men" as Archibald MacLeish puts it. MacLeish sees Pound there as "a conscious mind capable of the most complete human awareness . . . incarcerated among minds which are not conscious and cannot be aware," in an enforced association which "produces a horror which is not relieved either by the intelligence of doctors or by the tact of administrators or even by the patience and kindliness of the man who suffers it."

Yet, the plea for Pound's freedom runs constantly among those aware of his situation. In the New Directions booklet of tributes to Pound on his 70th birthday, Hemingway wrote,

> . . . Will gladly pay tribute to Ezra, but what I would like to do is get him the hell out of St. Elizabeth's, have him given a passport and allow him to return to Italy where he is justly valued as a poet. I believe he made bad mistakes in the war in continuing to broadcast for that sod Mussolini after we were fighting him. But I also believe he has paid for them in full and his continued confinement is a cruel and unusual punishment.

It is believed by some that the insanity verdict was a convenient "out" for the authorities. Hugh Kenner, in *Poetry,* November, 1952, wrote that "it has prevented the ideas expressed in the broadcasts from being inspected," that Pound has recited those ideas in prose and poetry for many years, and that his war-time gestures are intelligible only to those who have studied closely his Cantos and his essays on reading and culture. An inspection of Pound's Italian broadcasts (available on microfilm from the Library of Congress) does reveal what MacLeish has called the strident raging of the Cantos. But Robert Fitzgerald observed that few people seem to have read the transcripts of the talks

> . . . and I imagine few would care to . . . I could take a great deal of rage against the snakes of finance and I could well see the point of scorn for Roosevelt's public insincerities. Even anti-Semitism could be forgiven if it were what it had seemed to me in Pound before—an almost innocent vice partly echoing the Potash and Perlmutter era of comedy in America. But it was not like that, nor were the other contents in general anything but chaotic and unworthy. . . . I think that Pound at 20 or 30 would have thought hanging an entirely appropriate reward for the author of those radio scripts!

Pound's economic theories, the flow of his radio talks and the blood of his Cantos, originate from the Social Credit plan of Major C. H. Douglas and the doctrine of "free money" of Silvio Gesell. Gesell (1862-1930) wished to eliminate non-labor incomes, such as interest and rent. He proposed issuing "shrinking money" (*Schwundgeld*) which would weekly lose 0.1 percent of its face value, under a purchasing power control. Thus, such money could not be withheld from the market; it would cease to draw primary interest and become free. Douglas blamed our poverty-in-the-midst-of-plenty and the boom-depression cycles on the control of production and credit by a few financiers. Let us, he said, form one great holding company of securities, the United States, Inc., for example, compute the total national wealth, and, upon this, declare to all citizens a certain national dividend to be paid monthly. With the control of prices, wages, profits, with the consumers' demands parallel with production, the national dividend becomes the difference between production and consumption. Establish an equitable distribution of social credit; maintain private enterprise under a controlled profit system.

The two theories (in their more complex and detailed forms) became part of Pound's poetry. Our major problem, he says, is that of distribution. In 1930 in his *ABC of Economics,* he called for "the shortening of the working day . . . to keep credit distributed among a greater part of the population. . . . It is not the whole answer." He described the place of control of credit as

> . . . a dark room back of a bank, hung with deep purple curtains. No one must see what happens. What happened in the Bank of the USA before Mr. Van Buren set up an Independent government treasury? . . . Inflation for the benefit of the few.

He defined himself as a Jeffersonian republican: ". . . you can throw in Confucius and Van Buren, but you must distinguish between 1820 and 1930 and you must bring your Jefferson up to date." His preconception of democracy

> . . . as it existed in the minds of Jefferson and Van Buren, is that the best men . . . will take the trouble to place their ideas and policies before the majority with such clarity and persuasiveness that the majority will accept their guidance. . . . The preconception of let us say the Adamses, or aristodemocratic parties is that privilege, a little of it, will breed a sense of responsibility. . . . It seems fairly proved that privilege does NOT breed a sense of responsibility. . . . 95 percent of all privileged classes seem to believe that the main use of privileges is to be exempt from responsibility. . . . Obviously no best, no even good governing class can be spineless . . . "good" must include a capacity for action, some sense of relation between action and mere thought or talk.

As others cling to parts of his ideas, ignoring the disagreeable elements, so Pound clung to parts of Mussolini while apparently ignoring his baser actions. Pound frequently quoted Mussolini's prepower protest, "we are tired of a government in which there is no responsible person having a hind name, a front name, and an address," a point we might make good use of today. He printed on his letterheads the dictator's maxim, "Liberty is not a right but a duty." Admiring the ostensible encouragement Mussolini gave artists, Pound settled in Italy. From Rapallo for 20 years he was, as Yvor Winters says,

> . . . the most influential critic in American letters, so far as practical results were concerned; and when he was replaced, it was by his disciple Eliot, who did little save restate his ideas in a more genteel style.

"Am I American?" he wrote to Hubert Creekmore.

> . . . Yes, and bugger the present state of the country, the utter betrayal of the American Constitution, the filth of the Universities and the . . . system of publication whereby you can buy Lenin, Trotsky (the messiest mutt of the lot), Stalin for 10 cents and 25 cents, and it takes *seven* years to get a set of John Adams at about 30 dollars.

Long before his radio talks, Pound had spoken against

> . . . advocating fascism in and for America . . . I think the American system *de jure* is probably quite good enough, if there were only 500 men with guts and the sense to *use* it, or even with the capacity for answering letters, or printing a paper.

Apparently he had no idea that what he was doing would get him into trouble. He did not swerve from his belief that he was

> . . . only trying to tell the people of Europe and America how they could avoid war by learning the facts about money.

Pound easily could have become an Italian citizen, saving himself from later grief. But regularly he went to the American embassy to maintain his United States citizenship; he wanted, he says, to reaffirm his faith in the Constitution. Early in 1942 he made an attempt to get on the diplomatic train that took Americans from Italy to Lisbon for passage to the United States, but he was refused permission to join the group. Consequently, he remained in Rapallo. He says he was asked by the Italians if he would make some broadcasts. Anything that would save mankind was worth a try. He maintains that he was not forced to speak, that "no scripts were prepared for me by anybody, and I spoke only when I wanted to." At the beginning of each talk it was stated that he had no connection with the Italian government, that he was speaking only as an American citizen. He wanted to save the Constitution, to warn the people against usurers who, he said, destroy us.

His radio talks fit a description Yeats gave the Cantos.

> . . . nervous obsession, nightmare, stammering confusion; he is an economist, poet, politician, raging at malignants with inexplicable characters and motives, grotesque figures out of a child's book of beasts.

(Like *Ulysses,* the Cantos are based upon characters from history and fiction, upon an economy, motives, politics, all explicable within the poem's massive epic organization). When he was brought to the United States in an Army C-54 on November 18, 1945, he declared:

> If freedom of speech doesn't apply on the radio—in an age of radio . . . I'd die for an idea all right, but to die for an idea I've forgotten is too much. Does anyone have the faintest idea what I said?

That is, he did not realize he had said anything to arrest him for.

He had gone to the authorities in Italy in 1945 to tell them he heard they were looking for him. After some deliberation and incredulity, they accepted him as a prisoner. The report on his confinement at Pisa, where *The Pisan Cantos* had their birth, is best found in the Cantos themselves and in "The Background of *The Pisan Cantos*" by David Park Williams (*Poetry,* January, 1949) who was a literate guard at the Disciplinary Training Center where Pound was interned from May through October, 1945. The Center possessed a half dozen cages and sixty "boxes" which served as cells for "incorrigibles." Dangerous prisoners, such as the Lane gang members (Canto LXXIV), were placed in cages made of heavy wire, "enabling guards," Williams says, "to keep a 24-hour watch on those within." Apparently, the Army feared that Italian fascists would attempt a rescue of Pound, for a special cage was built for him—the "gorilla cage" of Canto LXXXIII.

"Ha, I was a dangerous criminal!" Pound said later.

. . . They thought I was a dangerous wild man and were scared of me. I had a guard night and day and when they built a cage out of iron mats from airplane runways and put me in the cage for the merriment of all, they posted a guard outside. Soldiers used to come up to the cage and look at me. Some of them brought me food. Old Ez was a prize exhibit.

He slept on the cement floor of the cage ("so kissed the earth after sleeping on concrete"). Tar paper was spread across the top to keep off the sun; he was given a pup tent to rig up inside the bars at night. The closing couplet of *The Pisan Cantos* thus takes on poignancy:

> If the hoar frost grip thy tent
> Thou wilt give thanks when night is
> spent.

No one ever tried to rescue Pound.

Much of *The Pisan Cantos* describes the scene: the barbed-wire enclosure, the constant figures of the guards, the trainees (as the prisoners were called) punished with close-order drill after dark (they were given 14 hours of training daily), "sweatin' it out to the bumm drum" of the prison band with guards on horseback keeping watch over it "as the young horse whinnies against the tubes." Pound clung to a worn volume of Confucius. He read hour upon end, "or simply sat," Williams says, "and combed his ragged beard, watching the Pisa road where passers-by and occasional white oxen were visible"—

> and there was a smell of mint under
> the tent flaps
> especially after the rain
> and a white ox on the road toward Pisa
> as if facing the tower
> dark sheep in the drill field and on wet
> days were clouds
> in the mountain as if under the guard
> roosts.          (Canto LXXIV)

Because of his poor health, Pound was moved from the cage after a few weeks to a pyramidal tent in the medical area, where he spent most of the summer and part of the fall of 1945. A prisoner gave him a packing-case for a table and there he was able to write. No one was allowed to speak to him at any time. But some did:

> and the greatest charity
> to be found among those who have not
>     observed regulations.

*     *     *

> They didn't know what to do with me, so they put old Ez in a cage and flew him back to the United States. . . . They kept me in confinement on a starvation diet when I first got here, and I didn't see the sun for months.

He was arraigned for treason based on opinions aired via radio—the first American ever to be so charged. He called it a "damned fool idea" that he had betrayed his country; he was, he insisted, bent upon saving it.

That insistence became part of a nine-sentence report by four psychiatrists, three for the government, one retained by Pound's defense, which declared him mentally incompetent—his "self-appointed mission" to "save the Constitution." The report spoke of his "uncertain living," his being "eccentric," his "advancing years," called him "abnormally grandiose," referred to his personality's "further distortion"—in effect, a good description of the independent artist. The report was considered valid and Pound was delivered to St. Elizabeth's Hospital in Anacostia. He was at first placed with the criminally insane in the violent ward. He later said:

> I met a very pleasant chap. We had many interesting conversations. He seemed no crazier than I. When I found out that he had been committed for killing his wife, I reconsidered my position.

At length, he was shifted to a more tranquil section, and there he remains.

For eleven years he has held his own court where he has been able, primarily in warm weather when he has been permitted afternoons outside the building (but never outside the hospital grounds) if accompanied by his wife. The Pounds have been married 43 years; Mrs. Pound's maiden name was, seriously and perhaps as symbolic and fanciful as anything in the Cantos, Dorothy Shakespear. She never misses a day at the hospital. When she arrives, Pound greets her with a wave and a kiss on her cheek.

And there, in a loose sweatshirt, an old GI overcoat, baggy trousers, heavy white socks, bedroom slippers, long underwear showing at his ankles, Pound sits on a chair warm afternoons on the wide, lush, and sweeping lawns of the grounds and peers at his visitors from beneath a green eyeshade. For his 71 years he is vigorous, still rough-bearded, still much as Eliot described him in 1946: " . . . his restless energy—in which it was difficult to distinguish the energy from the restlessness and the fidgets . . . a kind of resistance against growing into any environment." Actually, he has the problem of too many visitors who seek advice, aid, answers, literary judgments, and just the thrill of looking at him. Evidently, rather than spend time with the planned intellectual games of the hospital, he has chosen to work on such matters as his *The Classic Anthology Defined by Confucius,* published in 1954, and on further Cantos (*Section: Rock-Drill*) and translations.[1] In an effort to organize his thinking, he has concentrated a good deal on chess.

As far back as 1949 Dr. Frederic Wertham, author of *The Show of Violence* and other psychiatric studies of criminal insanity,

> . . . proved to the satisfaction of my own scientific conscience and that of many of my colleagues that according to the very statement given out by the authorities Ezra Pound was not legally insane and did not have any major disease which would render him legally insane.

And in the *American Journal of Psychotherapy,* Dr. Wertham further explored the insanity decision: in Italy, Pound was declared "sane and able to stand trial for treason" by Army psychiatrists; if he had been tried, by now he would have served his sentence and would have been released along with Axis Sally and the others.

---

[1] His translation of Sophocles' *The Women of Trachis* is being published this week (New Directions; $3).

Ironically, Pound's possibilities of being set free were probably damaged by his having received the Bollingen Award for *The Pisan Cantos*. A furor arose, not only among those preoccupied with literature, but also from housewives who wanted him hanged and businessmen who would have him shot—as well as from readers who fought to shed their tears over him. The Fellows of the Library of Congress, who made the award, were called fascists and "new authoritarians"—T. S. Eliot, one of the Fellows, was blamed for controlling the committee's votes, although as Malcolm Cowley pointed out (in *The New Republic*), Eliot "neither nominated the *Pisan Cantos* for the prize nor argued that it was the best book to choose; he merely cast one vote for it among eleven." The question of the separation of poet from his work flamed again. One of the Fellows of the Library asserts that "Our job wasn't to pass on the question of Pound's loyalty; we were giving a prize for a book of poems." Cowley further stresses the Fellows' view that other virtues exist as well as the patriotic: "Originality, learning, sharpness of image, purity of phrase and a strict literary conscience . . . and they are present in Pound's work along with his contemptible politics." By giving him the prize, the Fellows were defending, they insist, "that objective perception of value on which any civilized society must rest."

The battle spread to the Congress, where a Representative was busy calling modern art Communistic (the Communists call it capitalistic and decadent). An investigation of the Bollingen Award was demanded. Now the Library of Congress has been forced to cancel not only the prize in literature, but also its awards in music and art. As Cowley remarks:

> . . . The little American republic of letters is under attack by pretty much the same forces as those to which the Russian writers have already yielded: that is, by the people who prefer slogans to poetry and national self-flattery to honest writing.

Pound makes his own plea in one of the most touching and beautiful, and most quoted, of his *Pisan Canto* pasages:

> 'Master thyself, then others shall thee beare'
>     Pull down thy vanity
>  Thou art a beaten dog beneath the hail,

A swollen magpie in a fitful sun,
Half black half white
Nor knowst'ou wing from tail
Pull down thy vanity
   How mean thy hates

Fostered in falsity,
   Pull down thy vanity,
Rather to destroy, niggard in charity,
Pull down thy vanity,
   I say pull down.
But to have done instead of not doing
   this is not vanity
To have, with decency, knocked
That a Blunt should open
   To have gathered from the air a live tradition
or from a fine old eye the unconquered flame
This is not vanity.
   Here error is all in the not done,
all in the diffidence that faltered.

In 1955, Giovanni Papini sent a note to Ambassador Luce:

In the very moment when the chiefs of the Kremlin are sending back pardoned German war criminals, we cannot believe that the descendants of Penn and of Lincoln, of Emerson and of Walt Whitman, wish to be less generous than the successors of Lenin and Stalin.

"This would be a good year," Hemingway said, "to release poets." He said it in 1954.

## *Ezra Pound May Escape Trial and Be Allowed to Go to Italy*

### U. S. Awaits Mental Report on Poet for Policy Guide on Treason Charges

WASHINGTON, April 1—The Justice Department is giving consideration to dropping the treason charges against Ezra Pound, the poet, with a view to letting him return to Italy.

Attoiney General William P. Rogers disclosed this today in answer to a question at his news conference. He said Pound's fate depended upon new diagnoses by doctors at Saint Elizabeth's Hospital here, where the writer is confined as insane.

Pound, regarded by many critics as among the greatest American poets, was indicted for treason because of pro-Fascist activities in Italy during World War II. He was brought back to this country for trial, but psychiatrists found him unable to stand trial because he was "of unsound mind."

Under law, Pound would remain in the hospital until "cured" and able to stand trial. Doctors have recently expressed doubt, Mr. Rogers said today, that he will ever be competent to stand trial.

The Attorney General then put this rhetorical question:

"Is there any point in keeping him in there if he never can be tried?"

Indications are that any action will await a final decision by the Saint Elizabeth's doctors. If they say Pound will always be mentally incompetent, Mr. Rogers may then move to quash the long-standing indictment.

At that point Pound would apparently be under no legal compulsion to remain in Saint Elizabeth's. His "friends and supporters," Mr. Rogers suggested, could then arrange with the hospital to have him moved to Italy.

Pound's supporters have included a number of leading poets and other writers in this country and abroad. Robert Frost, who has played a prominent part in the campaign for his release, has called at the Justice Department to discuss the case. T. S. Eliot and Ernest Hemingway have written on Pound's behalf.

Pound, who is now 72 years old, had lived in Europe for forty years when he was returned here in 1945. His last home was in Rapallo, on the Italian Riviera.

Much of Pound's poetry has been violently anti-Semitic. His activities during World War II included anti-American broadcasts for the Mussolini Government of Italy.

Because of his politics—personally and in his poems—Pound has always been a controversial figure, even in literary circles.

In 1949, while he was in Saint Elizabeth's, he was awarded the $1,000 Bollingen Prize for the best poetry published by an American during the previous year. The award was for his "Pisan Cantos," an epic poem expressing, among other things, his strong political views.

Strong attacks were made on the Library of Congress, which sponsored the prize. In the end, selection of the Bollingen Prize winners was shifted from the library to Yale University.

Pound is said to be in good physical condition. He has often expressed a desire to return to Italy.

*The Nation,* April 19, 1958 (an editorial)

# What the Pound Case Means

A new phase has arrived in the career of Ezra Pound. One of the great poets of the age, this violent thinker who broadcast for Mussolini during the last war and whose anti-Semitism is one of the running sores of modern letters, may be about to go free. In a mental hospital in Washington, D.C., since 1945, he has been saved from trial for treason only by his paranoiac condition. Now a motion to free him has been filed in Federal District Court and, according to the United Press, there were indications that the Department of Justice will not seriously oppose the move.

We believe that Pound should be set free, unless his psychosis is so deep that continued commitment is advisable. We are opposed to capital punishment, and generally to life imprisonment as well. Confinement in St. Elizabeth's has not kept Pound from making disciples like John Kasper or lessened the subtler appeal of his reactionary attitudes for many intellectuals moved first of all by his verse, his passionate prose style, or the penetrating truths so often found side by side with the non sequiturs and foulnesses scattered through his writings. Moreover, the treason indictment was for specific wartime acts, not for his ideas or prejudices. Bloodier war criminals have been freed; we have had political ritual-killings enough for one generation.

It will be a triumph of democracy if we set Pound free, not because he is a martyr, but because a sick and vicious old man—even if he were not the brilliant poet he is, with a luminous side that all but transcends his faults—has his rights too. In Italy he may yet write a few more beautiful pieces, and in that cracked but crystal mirror of his hold up to us once more the image of a civilization that too often drives its best creators into self-exile and political horror.

# U. S. Asked to End Pound Indictment

## Court Told Poet's Insanity Is Incurable— Wife Would Take Him Back to Italy

by ANTHONY LEWIS

WASHINGTON, April 14—Attorneys for Ezra Pound moved today for dismissal of the treason indictment that has been pending against him since 1945.

The motion was supported by an affidavit from Dr. Winfred Overholser, Superintendent of St. Elizabeth's Hospital, the Government mental institution where the poet is confined. Dr. Overholser said:

¶Pound is "permanently and incurably insane," will never be competent to stand trial and "will die insane in St. Elizabeth's Hospital without trial of the charges against him if the indictment remains pending."

¶There is a "strong probability" that the crime charged to Pound —pro-Fascist broadcasts from Italy during World War II—"was the result of insanity," and it is doubtful that any prosecution "could show criminal responsibility."

¶If the indictment is dismissed, Dr. Overholser will recommend release of the poet in the custody of his wife.

"Further confinement can serve no therapeutic purpose," Dr. Overholser said. "It would be a needless expense and burden upon the public facilities of the hospital." He said the poet was "not a dangerous person and his release would not endanger the safety of other persons."

In addition to this psychiatric support, the motion advanced literary grounds to drop the treason charges. These came in a statement by Robert Frost, the poet who has headed an informal committee of literary figures seeking Pound's release.

"None of us can bear the disgrace of our letting Ezra Pound come to his end where he is," Mr. Frost said.

Mr. Frost attached to his statement comments on behalf of Pound by other writers. These included John Dos Passos, Van Wyck Brooks, Marianne Moore, Ernest Hemingway, Carl Sandburg, W. H. Auden, T. S. Eliot and Archibald MacLeish.

Mr. Hemingway wrote:

"Will gladly pay tribute to Ezra, but what I would like to do is get him to hell out of St. Elizabeth's."

Today's motion was filed by Thurman Arnold of Washington on behalf of Mrs. Pound. It said that she proposes to apply for the poet's release in her custody "with bond under such terms and conditions as will be appropriate to the public good and the best interests and peace of mind of the defendant."

Indications are that Pound would be taken back to Italy, where he had lived for twenty years before World War II. He has told visitors at the hospital that he would like to go back to Italy.

The broadcasts that resulted in Pound's indictment began in late 1941 and continued through 1943. They were mixtures of colloquial, almost homespun, political comment, abstruse allusions, anti-semitism. On Jan. 29, 1942, for example, Pound said:

"The United States has been for months and illegally at war through what I consider to be the criminal acts of a President whose mental condition was not, so far as I could see, all that could or should be desired of a man in so responsible a position or office."

In 1943 Pound was indicted in absentia, and in 1945 he was taken into custody in Italy and returned to this country for trial.

Four psychiatrists, including Dr. Overholser, examined Pound and found him insane. A jury entered a formal verdict to that effect, and he was committed to St. Elizabeth's.

Whether the motion for dismissal of the indictment succeeds now will depend in large part on the attitude of the Department of Justice.

At a press conference two weeks ago, Attorney General William P. Rogers said: "Is there any point in keeping him there if he never can be tried?"

When addressing to the Court a motion to dismiss
the indictment against Ezra Pound, Pound's
Counsel submitted this statement from Robert Frost:

UNITED STATES DISTRICT COURT
FOR THE DISTRICT OF COLUMBIA

UNITED STATES of AMERICA
v.
EZRA POUND, Defendant

Criminal No. 76028

# Statement of Robert Frost

I am here to register my admiration for a government that can
rouse in conscience to a case like this. Relief seems in sight for
many of us besides the Ezra Pound in question and his faithful
wife. He has countless admirers the world over who will rejoice
in the news that he has hopes of freedom. I append a page or so of
what they have been saying lately about him and his predicament.
I myself speak as much in the general interest as in his. And I feel
authorized to speak very specially for my friends, Archibald Mac-
Leish, Ernest Hemingway and T. S. Eliot. None of us can bear
the disgrace of our letting Ezra Pound come to his end where he
is. It would leave too woeful a story in American literature. He
went very wrongheaded in his egotism, but he insists it was from
patriotism—love of America. He has never admitted that he went
over to the enemy any more than the writers at home who have
despaired of the Republic. I hate such nonsense and can only listen
to it as an evidence of mental disorder. But mental disorder is
what we are considering. I rest the case on Dr. Overholser's pro-
nouncement that Ezra Pound is not too dangerous to go free in
his wife's care, and too insane ever to be tried—a very nice discrimination.

Mr. Thurman Arnold admirably put this problem of a sick man being held too long in prison to see if he won't get well enough to be tried for a prison offense. There is probably legal precedent to help toward a solution of the problem. But I should think it would have to be reached more by magnanimity than by logic and it is chiefly on magnanimity I am counting. I can see how the Department of Justice would hesitate in the matter from fear of looking more just to a great poet than it would be to a mere nobody. The bigger the Department the longer it might have to take thinking things through.

s/ Robert Frost
Robert Frost

*John Dos Passos:*
"I certainly think he [Pound] should be released in the custody of his wife."
*Van Wyck Brooks:*
"I would gladly sign any petition for the release of Ezra Pound."
*Marianne Moore:*
"Yes indeed. I feel strongly that it is stagnant and unrealistic of us not to secure the release of Ezra Pound from St. Elizabeth's."
*Ernest Hemingway:*
"Will gladly pay tribute to Ezra but what I would like to do is get him the hell out of St. Elizabeth's . . ."
*Carl Sandburg:*
". . . they ought to let him out now; he's had enough."
*W. H. Auden:*
"There are very few living poets, even if they are not conscious of having been influenced by Pound, who could say, 'My work would be exactly the same if Mr. Pound had never lived.' "
*T. S. Eliot:*
"I believe that I have in the past made clear enough my personal debt to Ezra Pound during the years 1915-22. I have also expressed in several ways my opinion of his rank as a poet, as a critic, as impresario of other writers, and as pioneer

of metric and poetic language. His 70th birthday is not a moment for qualifying one's praise, but merely for recognition of those services to literature, for which he will deserve the gratitude of posterity, and for appreciation of those achievements which even his severest critics must acknowledge."

*Archibald MacLeish:*

"Every year since I began teaching at Harvard and for long years before that I have been more impressed by the extraordinary vitality of Pound's work. Most work ages with time. His doesn't. It keeps the hard sharp glitter—the cutting edge."

*Robert Fitzgerald:*

"Ezra Pound's place in the story of poetry is not in question, and with every year, it becomes more discriminated and understood. . . . It goes without saying that all of us who practice the art of poetry are indebted to him."

*Allen Tate:*

"Pound is a great poet *in petto,* and an even greater instigator of literary enthusiasms and schools."

*Dag Hammarskjold:*

"Modern art . . . makes us seers—seers like Ezra Pound when, in the first of his Pisan Cantos, he senses 'the enormous tragedy of the dream in the peasants' bent shoulders.' Seers— and explorers—these we must be if we are to prevail."

*Richard H. Rovere:*

"The main thing about Ezra Pound is that he is a poet of towering gifts and attainments. Poetry is not a horse race or any other sort of competition, and it is silly to argue over which poet runs the fastest, jumps the highest, or dives the deepest. Still, a respectable case could be made out to the effect that the century has produced no talent larger or more fecund than Pound's. Certainly the fit comparisons would be with no more than half a dozen other men who write in English. These, as the literary Establishment sees the matter today, would be T. S. Eliot, Yeats, Frost (some dissent here, probably), W. H. Auden, and Dylan Thomas; later on, some of these names may be removed and replaced by some from the second rank, such as Wallace Stevens, Robert Graves, Walter de la Mare,

Marianne Moore, William Carlos Williams, E. E. Cummings, and Robert Lowell.

"Pound's position is secure, not only because of the power of his own work but because of his service as a midwife to genius and as an influence on other poets. Not long ago, the government which detains Pound in St. Elizabeth's circulated abroad, as part of its effort to persuade the world that we Americans really care about the finer things, a flossy periodical in which it was asserted that Ezra Pound 'has done more to serve the cause of English poetry than anyone else alive.' (The article, by Hayden Carruth, a gifted critic, also said, 'It is hard to think of a good reason why Pound should not have his freedom immediately.') The statement on his service is broad but difficult to gainsay. Of the poets of comparable stature, at least half have at one time or another been Pound's disciples; others were greatly aided by him. The best known and most influential poem of our time, Eliot's *The Waste Land,* took the shape in which the world knows it under his expert hand. Eliot submitted it to Pound at many stages, and in its penultimate stage it was, according to Eliot, 'a sprawling, chaotic poem . . . which left Pound's hands, reduced to about half its size, in the form in which it appears in print.' The dedication of *The Waste Land* reads, 'For Ezra Pound—*il miglior fabbro.*' Pound deeply influenced Yeats in the later phases of Yeats' career. But for Pound, the recognition of Robert Frost would have come more belatedly than it did. It was Pound who first got Frost published in the United States and Pound also who found a London publisher for James Joyce. Amy Lowell, E. E. Cummings, and William Carlos Williams sat, often in extreme discomfort, at his feet. W. H. Auden is of a later generation, but he has asserted that 'there are few living poets . . . who could say, "My work would be exactly the same if Mr. Pound had never lived." ' "

*The New York Times,* Saturday, April 19, 1958

# Court Drops Charge Against Ezra Pound

by ANTHONY LEWIS

WASHINGTON, April 18—Treason charges against Ezra Pound were dismissed today, opening the way for the 72-year-old poet's return to Italy.

With the consent of the Government, Chief Judge Bolitha J. Laws of Federal District Court here threw out an indictment returned against Mr. Pound in 1945. The case was never tried because the poet was found insane.

Judge Laws acted on two psychiatric grounds—that Mr. Pound would in all likelihood never be mentally competent to stand trial and that the allegedly traitorous broadcasts he had made from Italy during World War II might have been the result of insanity.

Medical advice to this effect had come from Dr. Winfred Overholser, superintendent of St. Elizabeth's Hospital. That is the Federal mental institution where Mr. Pound has been confined since 1945.

Dr. Overholser said this afternoon that Mr. Pound would remain in the hospital until his family had made plans for him and until his affairs had been straightened out in St. Elizabeth's.

"He has a lot of papers and books to take care of in his room," Dr. Overholser said. "He's carried on an active correspondence."

The poet's wife, Mrs. Dorothy Shakespear Pound, who will be his legal guardian, indicated she would move for his release next week. In the meanwhile he is under no restraint, and in fact he went downtown this afternoon unattended by anyone from St. Elizabeth's.

The court hearing today was a brief, formal affair, but with an undertone of drama.

Mr. Pound sat in the back of the courtroom, dressed in a shabby blue jacket, a tan sport shirt with the tails not tucked in and blue slacks. His pockets were full of folded envelopes and other scraps of paper.

Mrs. Pound and their son, Omar, a teacher at Roxbury Latin School in Boston, were with him, as were a group of persons evidently among his literary admirers. Mr. Pound would say nothing to reporters except a firm "yes" when asked if he wanted to return to Italy. He posed for pictures after putting on a long yellow scarf with Oriental characters on it.

Mr. Pound's attorney, Thurman Arnold, spoke for a few minutes, chiefly about Dr. Overholser's medical findings. He said he represented not only Mrs. Pound but also "the world community of poets and writers" in seeking dismissal of the indictment.

The Justice Department's representative, United States Attorney Oliver Gasch, said the Government thought the motion was "in the interest of justice and should be granted." He told Judge Laws, among other things, that it would be "virtually impossible" to produce evidence of Mr. Pound's sanity during the war years in Italy at so late a date.

Judge Laws had presided at the earlier phases of the Pound case —his arraignment after return to this country, and his commitment following a jury verdict that he was insane. Today Judge Laws asked just a few questions and then issued his order.

Mrs. Pound, who had been sitting at the counsel table with Mr. Arnold, walked back and gave her husband a kiss.

The person most responsible for today's denouement was not in court. He is Robert Frost, the poet, who had waged a persistent public and private campaign during the last two years for Mr. Pound's release. Among other things Mr. Frost had called on Attorney General William P. Rogers.

# New Canto for a Poet

Ezra Pound's literary output has poured forth steadily and his literary reputation has flourished despite his confinement in St. Elizabeths Hospital in Washington.

The poet has been confined in the Federal mental institution since 1945. Yesterday, wartime treason charges against him were dropped, opening the way for his return to Italy. In winter months in St. Elizabeths he has somehow managed to make himself oblivious to the disturbed patients who share his ward and to the continuously blaring television set. He has worked with the utmost concentration on composing new poetry, making new translations, and revising and editing previous writing.

This time of year he works outdoors, in the shade of the beautiful trees at the hospital, which was formerly an arboretum.

Mrs. Pound, who lives near by, goes daily to his ward. Together they carry the two folding aluminum chairs he keeps under his bed to the lawn. There she helps him with correspondence and proof reading, and they share the lunch she brought in a paper bag. She is the former Dorothy Shakespear, a blue-eyed, tweedy Englishwoman.

They were married in 1914 and have one son, Omar, who teaches at Roxbury Latin School in Boston.

## TWO NEW BOOKS DUE

In recent months Mr. Pound has been working on proofs for two books scheduled for publication shortly. One, "Diptych," will be hand-printed and hand-bound in Italy in a limited, autographed edition for sale at $35 a copy. The other, "Pavannes and Divagations," will be published here by New Directions, which also plans to bring out a new master edition of Mr. Pound's "Cantos."

The sale of the author's books increases every year, his publisher reports. As a result, most of what he has written is still available in book form.

Ironically, much of the demand for Mr. Pound's writings comes from American colleges, which he damned contemptuously when he left this country in disgust in 1907.

Mr. Pound, a brilliant young man with bright red hair, had a talent for poetry and a flair for being eccentric in 1907. He had been born in Idaho, in 1885, educated at Hamilton College and the University of Pennsylvania, and had taught at Pennsylvania and Wabash College.

Except for two short visits, the expatriate did not return to the United States until he was brought back in 1945 to be tried for treason.

During his thirty-eight years in England, France and Italy, Mr. Pound acquired a formidable reputation as poet, editor, translator, critic and iconoclast.

His literary followers today include many who disapprove heartily of his wartime espousal of fascism, and anti-Semitism. They forgive or ignore his political behavior because of his earlier role as writer and instructor of writers, and his continuing mastery of poetic diction.

## POUND'S OWN THEORY

Mr. Pound himself, in his "ABC of Reading," said:

"You can spot the bad critic when he starts by discussing the poet and not the poem."

"Pisan Cantos," completed after Mr. Pound's commitment to St. Elizabeth's, was awarded in 1949 the $1,000 Bollingen poetry prize by the Library of Congress. A storm of public disapproval was provoked, and critics backed away from committing themselves on whether Mr. Pound's work was prizeworthy.

In succeeding years, however, words of praise of his literary merit have crept back into print. His "Section: Rock-Drill," a new series of Cantos published in 1956, was acclaimed, as was his free adaptation of Sophocles' "Woman of Trachis," published last year.

*The Washington Star,* April 30, 1958

# Ezra Pound Still Sees Mad World Out of Step

## Poet Proves Undaunted by 12 Years in St. Elizabeth's As He Visits Burdick

by MARY MCGRORY, Star Staff Writer

Ezra Pound yesterday paid a bread-and-butter call on one of his benefactors, Representative Burdick, Republican of North Dakota, and in a 75-minute discourse as disconnected and obscure as one of his cantos tried to explain the steps which led to his indictment as a traitor and his 12 years' confinement in St. Elizabeth's Hospital.

One thing was perfectly clear. The bearded 72-year-old poet who broadcast for the Fascist government in Italy during wartime, has not altered by one whit those virulent views which got him into trouble in the first place. He sees himself still as a maligned defender of the Constitution.

"When I was in the hell-hole (his name for St. Elizabeth's), I used to think there were 160 million worse cases outside," he said at one point. It was his first interview since a court action on April 18 simultaneously dismissed the indictment for treason and freed him from the hospital as hopelessly but harmlessly insane.

He is expected to return to Italy, where he lived for most of his 40-years', self-imposed exile.

Representative Burdick, a maverick in politics who has consistently defied his own party, last August introduced a bill in the

144

House Judiciary Committee to review the Pound case. Thereafter he requested a report on the matter from the Library of Congress. The huge white-haired 78-year-old lawmaker explained to reporters before his eccentric guest arrived that he has never read a line of Pound's poetry—"I like things that are clear"—and that his interest was "not in the man but in the thing."

"I'm against people being railroaded into insane asylums," he said. "There's no question the fellow was off, but that was no reason to lock him up without letting him talk."

Mr. Burdick, suffering from a broken arm, was painfully propped up on the sofa in the home of his recent bride at 1761 Forty-first Place S.E.

Mr. Pound, dressed in a short-sleeved, open-necked cotton shirt and green cotton trousers and half-laced brown shoes, fairly bounded into the room. Wringing Mr. Burdick's good hand, he beamed, "This is a historic occasion."

"You have a classical face," Mr. Burdick observed.

The poet wore around his neck a canvas bag for his two pairs of glasses. His curly gray hair and beard were unkempt. He had no objection to being photographed, volunteering that he was "more used to being fingerprinted."

He quickly established himself in an easy chair, explaining "I can't hold my head up for long. That is where Dr. Overholser is absolutely correct. I was too exhausted to think."

Lolling back, he fixed his glittering grey eyes on his host. "I might as well turn loose things you may not know," he began. "They're still running the old disc."

He flashed back to a moment in Venice in 1898 when he was with his great-aunt and had no bother "with passports and frontiers and all that malarkey." A sentence later, he was in Toulouse, date unspecified, trying to get back to London and a "dirty little squirt" in the consulate was telling him he had to go back to the United States.

"Confucius says it is the worst thing that could happen to a country when its rulers talk like that," he said.

"I must keep on the track," he murmured distractedly and switched to 1939, when Senator Wheeler told him that Roosevelt "had packed the Supreme Court and now he can declare anything constitutional."

"That is what led me to kidnap that microphone," he said.

Then he unleashed a torrent of praise for the philosophy of John Adams and for the works of Catherine Drinker Bowen, whose biographies of Adams and Sir Edward Coke, the British jurist, he regards as "worth all the history that is being taught in all the universities."

He spoke fondly of his grandfather, Thaddeus Colman Pound, a Representative from Wisconsin (1871-1882) and said "T. C. was asking for the same things I am asking for in very much the same style."

He said it would be a good thing if "some of the sanity of the Greenback Party could have been restored."

H. A. Sieber, author of the Library of Congress report on Pound, proffered a picture of the "cage" in which the poet was confined when first picked up by American troops near Pisa in 1945.

Mr. Pound said he thought the report should be widely circulated. He was told it was going to be put in the Congressional Record.

"What about the teeming animal life rushing up the Capitol steps? How about having it where they can get it? What about putting it on sale at the newsstands? There were never any copies at the consulates abroad, where they were trying to hold the expatriates together. I thought when Herbert Hoover came into the White House the prejudices against expatriates might diminish a little. I don't know how you feel about Herbert Hoover. Any man may make errors in his youth."

"I ought to keep quiet for a couple of weeks," he mused. "There are so many who speak for me."

"You know, Ike invited me to dinner once. Yes, when he was president of Columbia. I was a member of the Academy of Social and Political Sciences. He didn't know what he was signing. I was in the hell-hole at the time. The American Institute of Arts and Letters never had the guts to throw me out or send me notices."

"I am not anti-Semitic," he said. (Even those who hail Pound as the greatest poet blush for the anti-Semitism which is rife in his works.) "I have been making jokes about Jews all my life. Fifty years ago, we had jokes about the Scotch and the Irish and the Jews and the best stories you got were from the Jews."

## 12 YEARS OF SILENCE

He went on to describe abusively a Jewish visitor at St. Elizabeth's, then added, "But I would trust Mr. Cournos (never further identified) a damned sight more than Winston Churchill," he concluded.

He stopped abruptly and looked at the Representative. "I'm talking too much. I don't have to tell it all in one day. I can come back. But you've had a chance to talk as much as you like. It is what you're paid for. I've had the plug in for 12 years. When I was in the gorilla cage, the guard said, 'We've got a man here either for two hours or two months, but any man who talks to him gets the box.' Few men of letters have these opportunities."

"I thought I was being flown home to give information to the State Department. I could see why a lot of this stuff shouldn't go to the public, but why not give it to the State Department? I could have been of considerable use. In a conquered country, the essential thing is to separate the honest men. I was paid 300 lire (about 50 cents) for writing those broadcasts and 350 lire for registering them. Damned lies. I never told the troops not to fight. They were in it. What I am interested in is the American Constitution."

Why did he make the broadcasts?

Mr. Pound launched a bitter attack on former President Roosevelt, ending with "The mildest judgment of Roosevelt is that he was a fool."

## CAME BACK IN '39

Mr. Pound came back in 1939 "to stop the war," he said. "It was monstrous for Italy and the U. S. to be at war." He tried to return again in 1941, he said, and again in 1942 on a diplomatic train, hoping to stop Roosevelt from being elected again.

"When I tried to come back and fight the election," he said, "that is when they didn't want me. If I had been here, I would have been jailed."

Still talking, Mr. Pound took leave of his host, promising to return if invited.

Outside, he confided to reporters he didn't think "they ever would have let me out if they didn't think I would go back to Italy."

He was asked about an old friend, the completely non-political and much venerated poet, Robert Frost, whose intervention in the case last summer is largely credited with bringing about his release. Since 1946, such writers as Archibald MacLeish, Ernest Hemingway and T. S. Eliot have agitated tirelessly in his behalf.

"He ain't been in much of a hurry," Mr. Pound said dryly and headed back to St. Elizabeth's where he will presumably stay until arrangements are made for his return to Italy.

# Pound to Live With Daughter

MERANO, Italy, May 17 (AP)—The American poet, Ezra Pound, plans to return to Italy in July to live with his daughter and grandchildren in a castle, near here, according to his daughter, Mary. She is the wife of Prince Boris de Rachewiltz, a noted Egyptologist, who lives a few miles from this north Italian mountain town.

# Ezra Pound's Canto to Run in Yale Mag

NEW HAVEN, Conn., Nov. 21 (AP)—Ezra Pound will have his latest canto published in Yale University's literary magazine. This is believed to be the first time the controversial poet has submitted a new work directly to a student publication.

It will be the second canto by Pound to be published in America since he was released last April from St. Elizabeth's Hospital near Washington, D.C., when the government withdrew its wartime charges of treason.

The poet is living in Schloss Brunnenburg, near Tirolo, Italy, with his daughter. There he is reported at work on the Paridiso section of his cantos. The Yale magazine will publish Canto 100.

The upcoming issue—entitled "Ezra Pound: A New Montage"—will feature articles by a group of distinguished authors, scholars, poets and artists assessing Pound's contribution to modern poetry.

*Yale Literary Magazine,* December, 1958

# The Teacher

by Babette Deutsch

The major poets of the twentieth century have acknowledged publicly their debt to Pound, the teacher. Not all have been as explicit about it as the author of *The Waste Land* (and how much the rest of us could learn from the blue pencillings on the "sprawling chaotic" first draft of that poem by the *"miglior fabbro"!*). In any event, makers as diverse as Eliot, Yeats, and William Carlos Williams were tutored to some degree by this ruthless critic, this generous friend. And since Wallace Stevens spoke of Eliot as one of *his* masters, he must be counted among the many who profited indirectly from Pound's teachings. Indeed, there is probably no poet writing in English, and few writing in the other Western languages, who has not learned from this craftsman. There are, of course, also those who show the strength of his influence by rebelling against it.

Each poet, whether disciple or master, takes from the work of another the particular element that furthers his own poetic metabolism. There are certain features in Pound's finest poetry, in admonitions repeated in his prose writings, his letters, his talk, that all practitioners should digest. These lessons may be stated briefly. One, set down as early as 1913, though, through a series of accidents, published only in 1950, is that "Bad technique is 'bearing false witness.'" The artist is acutely conscious both of himself and of the majestic, terrible, sometimes comic, often beautiful universe in which he finds himself. The poet is more articulate than others about himself, the world, the relation between himself and what surrounds him. He tries to see truly, to speak truly about his own experience, big or little. That is how he brings order into confusion. That is how he is able to deal with what might otherwise destroy him. His truth helps us. But if he is a bad craftsman, a poor technician, he tells it in a garbled fashion: he bears false witness, injuring himself and his readers.

But how does a good craftsman work? That depends partly on whether he is more concerned with words as speech or words as song, whether he is most at home with visual images and metaphors, or is a master of wit. Pound has reminded us of these distinctions. Under any circumstances, two virtues seem essential to technical excellence. One is economy. This means absence of the superfluous; it does not necessarily mean absence of ornament. Another virtue is accuracy. This means the appropriate cadence as well as the appropriate words, and does not necessarily, though it may occasionally, mean the directness and unambiguousness of prose. Together, these make for the highly charged language that is the language of poetry. There have been earlier teachers: among them, Horace, Lu Chi, Coleridge, who gave similar good advice. It remained for Ezra Pound to give it in the language of our time to the poets of our time, so that, if civilization survives the militant madness now rampant, readers in later centuries will rejoice.

# APPENDICES

# Pound's Poetry

*Cantos,* New Directions, 1948

## XLV

With *Usura*
With usura hath no man a house of good stone
each block cut smooth and well fitting
that design might cover their face,
with usura
hath no man a painted paradise on his church wall
*harpes et luthes*
or where virgin receiveth message
and halo projects from incision,
with usura
seeth no man Gonzaga his heirs and his concubines
no picture is made to endure nor to live with
but it is made to sell and to sell quickly
with usura, sin against nature,
is thy bread ever more of stale rags
is thy bread dry as paper,
with no mountain wheat, no strong flour
with usura the line grows thick
with usura is no clear demarcation
and no man can find site for his dwelling.
Stone cutter is kept from his stone
weaver is kept from his loom
WITH USURA
wool comes not to market
sheep bringeth no gain with usura
Usura is a murrain, usura

155

blunteth the needle in the maid's hand
and stoppeth the spinner's cunning. Pietro Lombardo
came not by usura
Duccio came not by usura
nor Pier della Francesca; Zuan Bellin' not by usura,
nor was 'La Calunnia' painted.
Came not by usura Angelico; came not Ambrogio Praedis,
Came no church of cut stone signed: *Adamo me fecit.*
Not by usura St Trophime
Not by usura Saint Hilaire,
Usura rusteth the chisel
It rusteth the craft and the craftsman
It gnaweth the thread in the loom
None learneth to weave gold in her pattern;
Azure hath a canker by usura; cramoisi is unbroidered
Emerald findeth no Memling
Usura slayeth the child in the womb
It stayeth the young man's courting
It hath brought palsey to bed, lyeth
between the young bride and her bridegroom
                              *CONTRA NATURAM*
They have brought whores for Eleusis
Corpses are set to banquet
at behest of usura.

### from *Canto* LXXX

Oh to be in England now that Winston's out
  Now that there's room for doubt
    And the bank may be the nation's
    And the long years of patience
    And labour's vacillations
May have let the bacon come home,
      To watch how they'll slip and slide
      watch how they'll try to hide
        the real portent
    To watch a while from the tower
      where dead flies lie thick over the old charter
    forgotten, oh quite forgotten
    but confirming John's first one,
  and still there if you climb over attic rafters;
to look at the fields; are they tilled?
is the old terrace alive as it might be
with a whole colony
        if money be free again?
Chesterton's England of has-been and why-not,
or is it all rust, ruin, death duties and mortgages
and the great carriage yard empty
        and more pictures gone to pay taxes

  When a dog is tall but
  not so tall as all that
  that dog is a Talbot
    (a bit long in the pasterns?)
When a butt is ½ as tall as a whole butt
That butt is a small butt
    Let backe and side go bare
and the old kitchen left as the monks had left it
and the rest as time has cleft it.

[Only shadows enter my tent
    as men pass between me and the sunset,]

beyond the eastern barbed wire
  a sow with nine boneen
matronly as any duchess at Claridge's

and for that Christmas at Maurie Hewlett's
Going out from Southampton
they passed the car by the dozen
    who would not have shown weight on a scale
                    riding, riding
                    for Noel the green holly
    Noel, Noel, the green holly
    A dark night for the holly

That would have been Salisbury plain, and I have not thought of
    the lady Anne for this twelve years
        Nor of Le Portel
How tiny the panelled room where they stabbed him
      In her lap, almost, La Stuarda
    Si tuit li dolh ehl planh el marrimen
      for the leopards and broom plants

Tudor indeed is gone and every rose,
Blood-red, blanch-white that in the sunset glows
Cries: "Blood, Blood, Blood!" against the gothic stone
Of England, as the Howard or Boleyn knows.

Nor seeks the carmine petal to infer;
Nor is the white bud Time's inquisitor
Probing to know if its new-gnarled root
Twists from York's head or belly of Lancaster;

Or if a rational soul should stir, perchance,
Within the stem or summer shoot to advance
Contrition's utmost throw, seeking in thee
But oblivion, not thy forgiveness, FRANCE.

as the young lizard extends his leopard spots
    along the grass-blade seeking the green midge half an ant-size
and the Serpentine will look just the same
and the gulls be as neat on the pond
and the sunken garden unchanged

and God knows what else is left of our London
    my London, your London
and if her green elegance
  remains on this side of my rain ditch
  puss lizard will lunch on some other T-bone

sunset grand couturier.


*from* Canto **LXXXI**

Yet
Ere the season died a-cold
Borne upon a zephyr's shoulder
I rose through the aureate sky
        *Lawes and Jenkyns guard thy rest*
        *Dolmetsch ever be thy guest,*
Has he tempered the viol's wood
To enforce both the grave and the acute?
Has he curved us the bowl of the lute?
        *Lawes and Jenkyns guard thy rest*
        *Dolmetsch ever be thy guest*
Hast 'ou fashioned so airy a mood
    To draw up leaf from the root?
Hast 'ou found a cloud so light
    As seemed neither mist nor shade?

        Then resolve me, tell me aright
        If Waller sang or Dowland played.

    Your eyen two wol sleye me sodenly
    I may the beauté of hem nat susteyne

And for 180 years almost nothing.

Ed ascoltando al leggier mormorio
    there came new subtlety of eyes into my tent,
whether of spirit or hypostasis,
    but what the blindfold hides

or at carneval
    nor any pair showed anger
    Saw but the eyes and stance between the eyes,
colour, diatasis,
        careless or unaware it had not the
   whole tent's room
nor was place for the full Εἰδὼς
interpass, penetrate
    casting but shade beyond the other lights
       sky's clear
       night's sea
       green of the mountain pool
       shone from the unmasked eyes in half-mask's space.
What thou lovest well remains,
              the rest is dross
What thou lov'st well shall not be reft from thee
What thou lov'st well is thy true heritage
Whose world, or mine or theirs
         or is it of none?
First came the seen, then thus the palpable
   Elysium, though it were in the halls of hell,
What thou lovest well is thy true heritage


The ant's a centaur in his dragon world.
Pull down thy vanity, it is not man
Made courage, or made order, or made grace,
   Pull down thy vanity, I say pull down.
Learn of the green world what can be thy place
In scaled invention or true artistry,
Pull down thy vanity,
          Paquin pull down!
The green casque has outdone your elegance.

"Master thyself, then others shall thee **beare**"
   Pull down thy vanity
Thou art a beaten dog beneath the hail,
A swollen magpie in a fitful sun,
Half black half white
Nor knowst 'ou wing from tail
Pull down thy vanity
      How mean thy hates

Fostered in falsity,
           Pull down thy vanity,
Rathe to destroy, niggard in charity,
Pull down thy vanity,
           I say pull down.

But to have done instead of not doing
      this is not vanity
To have, with decency, knocked
That a Blunt should open
      To have gathered from the air a live tradition
or from a fine old eye the unconquered flame
This is not vanity.
      Here error is all in the not done,
all in the diffidence that faltered,

Transcript of Short Wave Broadcasts from Rome,
December 7, 1941–July 25, 1943, issued by U. S.
Federal Communications Commission.
Microfilm copy made in 1952 by Library of Congress

# Excerpts from Pound's Broadcasts

EDITOR'S NOTE: The transcripts of Pound's radio talks are available on microfilm at the Library of Congress. There is no question but that the transcript contains some minor errors. As Mr. H. A. Sieber points out in his "The Case of Ezra Pound: A Cause Célèbre Is Ended" (*The Washington Post and Times Herald,* Sunday, July 6, 1958), "There are, of course, many instances where Pound's rambling, often disconnected thoughts, liberally sprinkled with obscure literary, historical and personal references, must have baffled the Federal Communications Commission clerk who transcribed the monitored broadcasts."

ANNOUNCER: Rome Radio . . . following the tradition of Italian hospitality . . . has offered Dr. Ezra Pound the use of the microphone twice a week. It is understood that he will not be asked to say anything whatsoever that goes against his conscience, or anything incompatible with his duties as a citizen of the U.S.A.

*Jan. 29, 1942.* The United States has been for months, and illegally at war through what I consider to be the criminal acts of a President whose mental condition was not, so far as I could see, all that could or should be desired of a man in so responsible a position or office.

*Feb. 3, 1942.* You are at war for the duration of the Germans' pleasure. You are at war for the duration of Japan's pleasure. Nothing in the Western world, nothing in the whole of our occident can help you dodge that. Nothing can help you dodge it.

*February 26, 1942.* After years of robbing the country, dipping into the treasury, years of frothing at the mouth about Mussolini and Hitler,

162

in the middle of January Roosevelt comes out with a discourse and every single item in it that has a trace of sanity in it is is imitated from Mussolini or from Hitler. After twenty years of Judaic propaganda, Lenin and Trotsky stuff, crowding American history out of the schools, wild inferiority hate against Europe, dear old Delano comes out with a mixed bag in which two-thirds of the program is Fascist with, of course the essential part missing.

*March 8, 1942.* I lose my thread at times, so much that I can't count on anyone's mind. Truth, as they call it, in discourse.

*April 16, 1942.* For the United States to be making war on Italy and on Europe is just plain damn nonsense, and every native-born American of American stock knows that it is plain downright damn nonsense. And for this state of things Franklin Roosevelt is more than any other one man responsible.

*April 23, 1942.* I ask whether the spirit of '76 is helped by a-floodin' the lower ranks of the Navy with bridge-sweepin's; whether war is won by mercantilist ethics and, in any case, whether men like Knox and Stimson and Morgenthau can be expected to fill the heart of youth with martial ardor and the spirit of sacrifice.

*May 10, 1942.* The next peace will not be based on international lending. Get that for one. The next peace will not be based on international lending, and England certainly will have nothing whatever to say about what its terms are. Neither, I think, will simple-hearted Joe Stalin, not wholly trusted by the kikery which is his master.

*May 26, 1942.* Every hour that you go on with this war is an hour lost to you and your children. And every sane act you commit is committed in homage to Mussolini and Hitler. Every reform, every lurch toward the just price, toward the control of a market is an act of homage to Mussolini and Hitler. They are your leaders however much you think you are conducted by Roosevelt or told by Churchill. You follow Mussolini and Hitler in every constructive act of your government.

*May 31, 1942.* The melting pot in America may have been a noble experiment, though I very much doubt it. At any rate it is lost.

*June 28, 1942.* You are not going to win this war. None of our best minds ever thought you could win it. You have never had a chance in this war.

*July 20, 1942.* You ought not to be at war against Italy. You ought not to [be] giving or ever have given the slightest or most picayune aid to any man or nation engaged in waging war against Italy. You are doing it for the sake of a false accountancy system.

*July 22, 1942.* Europe calling . . . Ezra Pound speaking! I hear that my views are shared, most of them, by a large number of my compatriots, so it would seem, or maybe an increasing number of my compatriots. And there is a comforting thought on a warm day in a fine climate. I should hate to think that all America had gone haywire. I should like to feel that the American race in North America, in the North American continent, had some wish towards survival. That they wanted there to be a United States of tomorrow. . . .

Well, you have been fed on lies, for 20 years you have been fed on lies, and I don't say maybe. And Mr. Squirmy and Mr. Slime are still feeding it to you right over the BBC radio, and every one of the Jew radios of Schenectady, New York and Boston—and Boston was once an American city; that was when it was about the size of Rapallo. . . .

And how much liberty have you got, anyhow? And as to the arsenal —are you the arsenal of democracy or of judeocracy? And who rules your rulers? Where does public responsibility end and what races can mix in America without ruin of the American stock, the American brain? Who is organized? What say have you in the choice of your rulers? What control of their policy? And who does own most of your press and your radio? E. P. asking you. . . .

*April 27, 1943.* I don't think there is any American law that permits you to shoot Nicholas Butler. It's a pity, but so it is no ex post facto laws are to be dreamed of. Not that Frankfurter or any other damn Jew cares a hoot for law, or for the American Constitution.

*May 4, 1943.* What are you doing in the war at all? What are you doing in Africa? Who amongst you has the nerve or the sense to do something that would conduce to getting you out of it before you are mortgaged up to the neck and over it? Every day of war is a dead day as well as a death day. More death, more future servitude, less and less of American liberty of any variety. . . .

# Bibliography

[Items marked by a single asterisk are ones which the editors consider important; those marked by a double asterisk, *extremely* important. Many of the former, of course, have been reprinted in this book. The latter were left out simply because permission to reprint them was not obtainable: *these should be reserved by the instructor for class use and be made required reading for all essays resulting from the use of this book.*]

# SECONDARY SOURCES

## ARTICLES

Adams, R. M. "A Hawk and a Handsaw for Ezra Pound," *Accent,* VIII (Summer, 1948), 205-214.

Alsterlund, B. "Newsmen and Their Wares," *Wilson Library Bulletin,* XVIII (September, 1943), 6.

"Awarded Bollingen Prize for Poetry," *Publishers' Weekly,* CLV (March 5, 1949), 1162.

Barnard, H. "Reply [to Peter Viereck]," *Commonweal,* LVI (May 30, 1952), 198-199.

*Barrett, William. "A Prize for Ezra Pound," *Partisan Review,* XVI (April, 1949), 344-347.

Benét, W. R. "Phoenix Nest," *Saturday Review of Literature,* XXXII (July 23, 1949), 28.

*Berryman, John. "The Poetry of Ezra Pound," *Partisan Review,* XVI (April, 1949), 377-394.

Blackmur, R. P. "Adjunct to the Muses' Diadem: A Note on Ezra Pound," *Poetry,* LXVIII (September, 1946), 338-347.

"Bollingen Prize in Poetry," *Annual Report, Library of Congress,* (June 30, 1949), 88-94.

Bottrall, Ronald. "Ezra Pound," *Adelphi,* XXVIII (Second Quarter, 1952), 618-23.

Brooks, V. "Religion of Art," *Saturday Review of Literature,* XXXIV (December 1, 1951), 13ff.

Burt, Struthers. "Pro Bollingen Bosh," *Saturday Review of Literature,* XXXII (August 27, 1949), 21-23.

Canby, H. S. "Ezra Pound," *Saturday Review of Literature,* XXVIII (December 15, 1945), 10.

*Carruth, Hayden. "The Anti-poet All Told; Ezra Pound and the Bollingen Award," *Poetry,* LXXIV (August, 1949), 274-285.

Cerf, Bennett. "The Case of Ezra Pound," *Saturday Review of Literature,* XXIX (March 23, 1946), 32-36, 49-53.

Cerf, Bennett and Lewis Gannett. "The Case of Ezra Pound," *Saturday Review of Literature,* XXIX (February 9, 1946), 26-27.

Cohane, J. J., Jr. "Poet Without a Country; Reply," *Commonweal,* XLI (November 10, 1944), 101.

*Cousins, Norman and Harrison Smith. "Ezra Pound and the Bollingen Award," *Saturday Review of Literature,* XXXII (June 11, 1949), 20-21.

*Cowley, Malcolm. "The Battle over Ezra Pound," *New Republic,* CXXI (October 3, 1949), 17-20.

Cowley, Malcolm. "Books and People," *New Republic,* CIX (November 15, 1943), 689.

Cowley, Malcolm. "Fox in Flight," *Furioso,* VI (Spring, 1951), 7-10.

Davis, Robert G. "The New Criticism and the Democratic Tradition," *The American Scholar,* XIX (Winter, 1949-1950), 9-19.

Davis, Robert G. "Pound: The Poem and the Poet," *New Leader,* (December 11, 1950), 17-18.

*Dillon, George. "A Note on the Obvious," *Poetry,* LXVIII (September, 1946), 322-325.

"Discussion," *New Republic,* CXXI (October 17, 1949), 4.

"Discussion," *Saturday Review of Literature,* XXXI (October 2, 1948), 21.

"Discussion," *Saturday Review of Literature,* XXXII (June 25, 1949), 26.

"Discussion," *Saturday Review of Literature,* XXIX (March 16, 1946), 32-36ff.

Dudek, Louis. "Correspondence," *Canadian Forum,* XXIX (November, 1949), 185-186.

Eberhart, Richard. "Pound's New Cantos," *Quarterly Review of Literature,* V, No. 2 (1949), 174-191.

*Eliot, T. S. "Ezra Pound," *Poetry,* LXVIII (September, 1946), 326-338.

Elliott, Robert C. "Moral Evil and Literary Value," Ohio State *Argo,* (Spring, 1951), 27-36.

*Evans, L. H. "The 1948 Library of Congress-Bollingen Award to Ezra Pound," *Saturday Review of Literature,* XXXII (July 2, 1949), 20-23.

Evans, O. W. "Poet Without a Country," *Commonweal,* XLI (October 20, 1944), 10-12ff.

Evans, O. W. "Poet Without a Country; Rejoinder," *Commonweal,* XLI (December 1, 1944), 171.

[Ezra Pound and the Bollingen Award] *Saturday Review of Literature,* XXXII (June 25, 1949), 26.

[Ezra Pound and the Bollingen Award] *Saturday Review of Literature,* XXXII (July 2, 1949), 24-26.

[Ezra Pound and the Bollingen Award] *Saturday Review of Literature,* XXXII (September 27, 1949), 21-23.

[Ezra Pound and the Bollingen Award] *Saturday Review of Literature,* XXXII (October 1, 1949), 22.

"Ezra Pound Judged Unsound, Committed to Mental Hospital," *Publishers' Weekly,* CXLIX (February 23, 1946), 1247.

"Ezra Pound Excluded from Anthology," *Publishers' Weekly,* CXLVIII (December 22, 1945), 2693-2694.

*Ferkiss, Victor L. "Ezra Pound and American Fascism," *Journal of Politics,* XVII (May, 1955), 173-197.

Friar, Kimon. "Politics and Some Poets," *New Republic,* CXXVII (July 7, 1952), 17-18.

Giovannini, Giovanni. "The Strange Case of Ezra Pound." *The New Times* (August 26, 1955), 2.

Glicksberg, Charles I. "Ezra Pound and the Fascist Complex," *South Atlantic Quarterly,* XLVI (July, 1947), 349-358.

Healy, J. V. "Addendum," *Poetry,* LXVIII (September, 1946), 347-349.

**Hillyer, Robert. "Treason's Strange Fruit; The Case of Ezra Pound and the Bollingen Award," *Saturday Review of Literature,* XXXII (June 11, 1949), 9-11ff.

**Hillyer, Robert. "Poetry's New Priesthood"; *Saturday Review of Literature,* XXXII (June 18, 1949), 7-9ff.

Hynes, Sam. "The Case of Ezra Pound," *Commonweal,* LXIII (December 9, 1955), 251-254.

Hume, Robert. "The Contribution of Ezra Pound," *English,* VIII (Summer, 1950), 60-65.

"I Will Not Go Mad," *Newsweek,* XXXIV (December 26, 1949), 35.

*Kenner, Hugh. "Gold in the Gloom," *Poetry,* LXXXI (November, 1952), 127-132.

Kenner, Hugh. "In the Caged Panther's Eyes," *Hudson Review,* I (Winter, 1949), 580-586.

Kenner, Hugh. "The Rose in the Steel Dust," *Hudson Review,* III (Spring, 1950), 66-124.

*LaZebnik, Jack. "The Case of Ezra Pound," *New Republic,* CXXXVI (April 1, 1957), 17-20.

*Lewis, Wyndham. "Ezra: The Portrait of a Personality," *Quarterly Review of Literature,* V, No. 2 (1949), 136-144.

*Marshall, Margaret. *"The Saturday Review* Unfair to Literature," *Nation,* CLXIX (December 17, 1949), 598-599.

Meyer, G. P. "Sage of Rapallo," *Saturday Review of Literature,* XXXIII (December 2, 1950), 24-25.

"News Notes: Award of the Bollingen Prize," *Poetry,* LXXIV (April, 1949), 56ff.

"No Treason Trial for Ezra Pound," *Nation,* CLXII (January 5, 1946), 3.

Norman, Charles (ed.). "Articles on Ezra Pound," *PM,* (November 1945).

O'Connor, W. V. "What Does Mr. Pound Believe?" *Saturday Review of Literature,* XXXI (September 4, 1948), 15-16.

Paige, D. D. "Letters of Ezra Pound," *Hudson Review,* III (Spring, 1950), 53-56.

Peel, R. "The Poet as Artist and as Citizen," *Christian Science Monitor Magazine Section* (December 9, 1950), 7.

"Portrait," *Saturday Review of Literature,* XXX (March 22, 1947), 10.

"Portrait," *Time,* LII (October 25, 1948), 110.

"Portrait," *Saturday Review of Literature,* XXXII (August 6, 1949), 109.

"Portrait," *Theatre Arts,* XXXIV (September, 1950), 35.

"Portrait," *Time*, LIV (August 29, 1949), 11.

"Portrait," *Saturday Review*, XXXV (February 2, 1952), 35.

"Pound Foolish," *Newsweek*, XXVII (Feb. 25, 1946), 29.

"Pound's Prize," *Scholastic*, LIV (March 2, 1949), 15.

*Rattray, David. "Weekend with Ezra Pound," *Nation*, CLXXXV (November 16, 1957), 343-345.

"Remember Ezra?" *Newsweek*, XXVI (December 3, 1945), 38ff.

Rosenfeld, Paul. "The Case of Ezra Pound," *American Mercury*, LVIII (January, 1944), 98-102.

Rovere, Richard. "The Question of Ezra Pound," *Esquire* (September, 1957). See also subsequent issues.

Schlauch, Margaret. "The Anti-humanism of Ezra Pound," *Science and Society*, XIII (Summer, 1949), 258-269.

"Seeker," *Time*, XLVI (December 10, 1945), 22.

Shapiro, Karl. "Letter," *The Baltimore Sun*, (February 25, 1949).

Sheerin, J. B. "The Pound Affair," *Catholic World*, CLXIX (August, 1949), 322-323.

Shirer, William L. "The American Radio Traitors," *Harper's Magazine*, CLXXXVII (October, 1943), 397-404.

Sieber, H. A. and Fleming, Rudd. "The Case of Ezra Pound: A Cause Célèbre Is Ended," *The Washington Post and Times Herald* (July 6, 1958), E 7.

Sillen, Samuel. "A Prize for Ezra Pound," *Masses and Mainstream*, II (April, 1949), 3-6.

Smith, Harrison. "End of Controversy," *Saturday Review of Literature*, XXXII (September 3, 1949), 23.

Smith, Harrison. "Strange Paradox," *Saturday Review*, XXXV (February 9, 1952), 20.

Tichenor, G. H. "This Man Is a Traitor," *PM*, (August 15, 1943), 3-5.

"To Define True Madness," *Canadian Forum*, XXIX (September, 1949), 125.

"Treason," *Time*, XLVI (Dec. 10, 1945), 22.

"Understanding the News," *Scholastic*, LIV (March 2, 1949), 15.

*[Various]. "The Question of the Pound Award," *Partisan Review*, XVI (May, 1949), 512-522.

*[Various]. "Further Remarks on the Pound Award," *Partisan Review*, XVI (June, 1949), 666-670.

Viereck, Peter. "Parnassus Divided," *The Atlantic Monthly*, CLXXXIV (October, 1949), 69-70.

*Viereck, Peter. "Pure Poetry, Impure Politics and Ezra Pound," *Commentary*, XI (April, 1951), 340-346.

Watts, H. H. "The Devices of Pound's Cantos," *Quarterly Review of Literature*, V, No. 2 (1949), 147-173.

Watts, H. H. "Philosopher at Bay," *Cronos*, II (March, 1948), 1-16.

Watts, H. H. "Pound's Cantos: Means to an End," *Yale Poetry Review*, No. 6 (1947), 9-20.

Wertham, Frederic. "For Ezra Pound's Release," *Saturday Review of Literature*, XXXIV (April 7, 1951), 22.

Wertham, Frederic. "Road to Rapallo: A Psychiatric Study," American Journal of Psychotherapy, pages 585-600, (1949).

*West, Ray. "Excerpts from a Journal; 1949," *Western Review*, XIV (Winter, 1950), 82, 151-159.

"Weston," *The New Yorker*, XIX (August 14, 1943), 16-17.

"What the Pound Case Means," *Nation*, CLXXXVI (April 19, 1958), 335.

Whittemore, Reed. "Pound on Pound," *Poetry*, LXXIII (November, 1948), 108-110.

*Williams, David P. "The Background of the *Pisan Cantos*," *Poetry*, LXXIII (January, 1949), 216-221.

Williams, W. C. "Some Notes toward an Autobiography," *Poetry*, LXXIV (May, 1949), 94-111.

"Wins Bollingen Prize," *Time*, LIII (February 28, 1949), 40.

"Your Witness: Ezra Pound," *Scholastic*, XLVIII (April 29, 1946), 20.

Zukofsky, Louis. "The Cantos of Ezra Pound," *The Criterion*, X (April, 1931), 424-440.

## BOOK REVIEWS OF THE PISAN CANTOS

Bogan, Louise. *The New Yorker*, XXIV (October 30, 1948), 107.

Deutsch, Babette. *The New York Herald Tribune* Weekly Book Review, (August 22, 1948), 7.

Ferril, T. H. *San Francisco Chronicle* (November 7, 1948), 11.

Fitzgerald, Robert. *New Republic,* CXIX (August 16, 1948), 21.

Frankenberg, Lloyd. *The New York Times* (August 1, 1948).

Humphries, Rolfe. *Nation,* CLXVII (September 25, 1948), 349.

Kennedy, Leo. *Chicago Sun* (August 9, 1948).

Martz, L. L. *The Yale Review,* XXXVIII, No. 5 (Autumn, 1948), 144.

O'Connor, W. V. *Saturday Review of Literature,* XXXI (September 4, 1948), 15.

Whittemore, Reed. *Poetry,* LXXIII (November, 1948), 108.

Williams, W. C. *Imagi* (Spring, 1949).

### BOOKS

Blackmur, R. P. *Language as Gesture.* (New York: Harcourt, Brace and Company, 1952).

Edwards, John H. (ed.) *The Pound Newsletter.* (Berkeley: University of California, 1954-55).

Edwards, John H. *A Preliminary Checklist of the Writings of Ezra Pound.* (New Haven: Kirgo-Books, 1953).

Eliot, T. S. *Ezra Pound, His Metric and Poetry.* (New York: Alfred A. Knopf, 1917).

Espey, John. *Ezra Pound's Mauberley.* (Berkeley and Los Angeles, California: University of California Press, 1955).

Gregory, Horace, and Marya Zaturenska. *A History of American Poetry 1900-1940.* (New York: Harcourt, Brace and Company, 1946).

Hoffman, Frederick J. *The Twenties.* (New York: Viking Press, 1955). ["The Text: Ezra Pound's *Hugh Selwyn Mauberley,*" pp. 36-46.]

Kenner, Hugh. *The Poetry of Ezra Pound.* (Norfolk, Conn.: New Directions, 1951).

Leary, Lewis (ed.) *Motive and Method in The Cantos of Ezra Pound.* (New York: Columbia University Press, 1954).

Leavis, F. R. *New Bearings in English Verse.* (London: Chatto and Windus, 1932).

*MacLeish, Archibald. *Poetry and Opinion: The Pisan Cantos of Ezra Pound.* (Urbana, University of Illinois Press, 1950).

MacLeish, Archibald. *A Time to Speak.* (Boston: Houghton-Mifflin Company, 1941).

*Norman, Charles (ed.) *The Case of Ezra Pound.* (New York: Bodley Press, 1948).

*[Various.] *Quarterly Review of Literature,* V, No. 2, 1949. [Ezra Pound Issue.]

Read, Sir H. E. *True Voice of Feeling.* (New York: Pantheon Press, 1953).

*Russell, Peter (ed.) *Ezra Pound.* (London: Peter Nevill, 1950), (Norfolk, Conn.: New Directions, 1950). Published also by New Directions as *An Examination of Ezra Pound.*

Shapiro, Karl. *Beyond Criticism.* (Lincoln, The University of Nebraska, 1953). ["Introduction," pp. 1-6.]

**Sieber, H. A. (ed.) *The Medical, Legal, Literary and Political Status of Ezra Weston [Loomis] Pound [1885-  ], Selected Facts and Comments.* (Washington, The Library of Congress Legislative Reference Service, March 31, 1958. Revised April 14, 1958).

Symposium on Pound in *New Masses,* c. 1945-46.

Tate, Allen. *The Forlorn Demon.* (Chicago, H. Regnery, 1953) ["Ezra Pound and the Bollingen Prize," pp. 156-160].

*[Various.] *The Case Against the Saturday Review of Literature.* (Chicago: [special issue of *Poetry*], 1949).

*Viereck, Peter. *Dream and Responsibility.* (Washington, D.C.: The University Press, 1953), "Pure Poetry, Impure Politics," pp. 3-22.

*Viereck, Peter. *Shame and Glory of the Intellectuals.* (Boston: The Beacon Press, 1952) ["Symbols: Hiss and Pound," pp. 304-309].

*Watts, Harold H. *Ezra Pound and the Cantos.* (Chicago: H. Regnery, 1952).

*Weyl, Nathaniel. *Treason: The Story of Disloyalty and Betrayal in American History.* (Washington, D. C.: Public Affairs Press, 1950) ["The Strange Case of Ezra Pound," pp. 400-411].

Williams, William Carlos. *The Autobiography of William Carlos Williams.* (New York: Random House, 1951).

*Yale Literary Magazine,* Special Issue, c. Fall, 1949 [*Shattering Review of Literature*].

Yeats, William Butler. *A Packet for Ezra Pound.* (Dublin, Ireland: The Cuala Press, 1929). Reprinted in *A Vision.* (London: Macmillan, 1937, and New York: Macmillan, 1938, 1956).

*Yale Literary Magazine,* Issue on Ezra Pound, December, 1958.

NEW YORK TIMES

"Ezra Pound, Back, Censures Bankers," April 21, 1939, Page 18, Col. 5.

"Ezra Pound, Wanted for Treason, Seized by American Forces Near Genoa in Italy," [illus.] May 6, 1945, Page 12, Col. 5.

"Ezra Pound Still Held," [in Italy] September 5, 1945, Page 18, Col. 2.

"Pound Coming Soon for Treason Trial," November 7, 1945, Page 10, Col. 2.

"Brought Back to Face Treason Charges," [illus.] November 19, 1945, Page 12, Col. 3.

"Pound Would Call Wallace, M'Leish," November 20, 1945, Page 11, Col. 1.

"Pound Awaits Treason Trial," November 25, 1945, Page 7, Col. 3, (IV).

"Ezra Pound Indicted," November 27, 1945, Page 10, Col. 7.

"Pound Pleads Innocent," November 28, 1945, Page 2, Col. 6.

"Ezra Pound Insane; Unfit to Be Tried," December 22, 1945, Page 1, Col. 7.

"Pound's Mind 'Unsound,' " February 14, 1946, Page 20, Col. 2.

*"Pound's Poems, Previously Barred by Cerf, to Go Into a New Edition of Anthology," March 14, 1946, Page 23, Col. 4.

"Round Two," March 31, 1946, Page 36, Col. 5, (VII).

*"Pound, in Mental Clinic, Wins Prize for Poetry Penned in Treason Cell [with statement of judges]," February 20, 1949, Page 1, Col. 6; Page 14, Col. 1-2.

*"Evaluating the Pound Award," [Letter by Adrienne Koch and W. M. Lowry] February 24, 1949, Page 22, Col. 7.

*"Poet Protests Award to Pound," [Letter of Gustav Davidson] March 3, 1949, Page 24, Col. 6.

"Would Sift Poetry Prize: Asks Congress Inquire into Ezra Pound Award," July 22, 1949, Page 10, Col. 2.

"Pound Prize Inquiry Set," August 8, 1949, Page 13, Col. 8.

"Savants . . . Defend . . . Award to . . . 'Pisan Cantos,' " August 12, 1949, Page 9, Col. 3.

"Poetry Award to Pound to Be Last by Library," August 20, 1949, Page 13, Col. 7.

"Cancellation of Prizes Protested," [Letter by Gustav Davidson] August 29, 1949, Page 16, Col. 7.

*Aline B. Louchheim. "The State and Art," September 4, 1949, Page 8, Cols. 1-3 (II)

"Inquest on Pound Award," October 13, 1949, Page 21, Col. 5.

"Wertham Assails Ezra Pound [Insanity] Ruling," November 27, 1949, Page 33, Col. 1, (I).

"L'Affaire Pound," January 1, 1950, Page 8, Col. 2 (VII).

"Yale to Take Over Bollingen Awards," February 14, 1950, Page 27, Col. 1.

*"Library [of Congress] Explains Bollingen Award," March 23, 1950, Page 27, Col. 1.

"Ezra Pound May Escape Trial," April 2, 1958, Page 16, Col. 5.

"U. S. Asked to End Pound Indictment," April 15, 1958, Page 19, Cols. 3-5.

"Court Drops Charges Against Ezra Pound," April 19, 1958, Page 1, Col. 1, Page 23, Cols. 6-7.

"New Canto for a Poet," April 19, 1958, Page 23, Cols. 6-7.

# PRIMARY SOURCES

## (*Works by Ezra Pound*)

### I. POETRY

*The Cantos of Ezra Pound.* (New York: New Directions, 1948).
*Cantos 1-71* and *74-84*.

(with Ernest Fenollosa) *"Noh."* (New York: New Directions, 1959).

*Personae: The Collected Poems of Ezra Pound.* (New York: Horace Liveright, 1926; reprinted with additional poems, New York: New Directions, 1949).

*The Pisan Cantos.* (New York: New Directions, 1948).

*Section: Rock-Drill: 85-95 de los cantares.* (New York: New Directions, 1956). *Cantos 85-95.*

*The Selected Poems of Ezra Pound.* (New York: New Directions, 1949).

*Thrones: 96-109 De Los Cantares.* (New York: New Directions, 1959). Cantos 96-109.

*The Translations of Ezra Pound.* (New York: New Directions, n.d. [1954]).

### II. PROSE

*ABC of Reading.* (London: G. Routledge and Sons, 1934; New Haven: Yale University Press, 1934; Norfolk, Conn.: New Directions, 1951?).

*America, Roosevelt and the Causes of the Present War.* (London: Peter Russell, Ltd., 1951).

*Culture.* (Norfolk, Conn.: New Directions, 1949).

"The Jefferson-Adams Correspondence," *The North American Review, CCXLIV* (Winter, 1937-1938), 314-324.

*Jefferson and/or Mussolini.* (London: Stanley Nott, Ltd., 1935; New York: Liveright, 1935).

*The Letters of Ezra Pound: 1907-1941,* D. D. Paige, ed. (New York: Harcourt, Brace and Company, 1950).

"Letters to a Young Poet from Ezra Pound," *Poetry,* LXXVI (September, 1950), 342-351.

*Literary Essays,* T. S. Eliot, ed. (Norfolk, Conn.: New Directions, 1954).

*Money Pamphlets.* 6 Vols. (London: Peter Russell, 1950-1952).

*Social Credit: An Impact.* (London, Stanley Nott, Ltd., 1935).

"A Social Creditor Serves Notice," *Fascist Quarterly,* II (1936), 492-499.

*The Unwobbling Pivot and the Great Digest.* (New York: New Directions, 1947).

*A Visiting Card.* (London: Peter Russell, Ltd., 1952).

# Topics for Research Exercises

[All of the topics below can be developed in 300-1000 words from the documents in this volume, but students should be encouraged to extend their investigation with the resources of the library.]

1. Write a chronological account of Pound's life from the time of his arrest in Italy to his release from the hospital. Keep it as factual as possible.

2. Papers and magazines are at times news-reporting media, at times opinion-forming ones. What attitude, if any, toward Pound does the coverage of these periodicals reveal?
   a) *Time*
   b) *The New York Times*

3. What is the nature of the argument between Mr. Saturday and Mr. Bollingen as developed by Archibald MacLeish? Use any other articles you find helpful in stating the issues.

4. Specify the nature of the various critical evaluations of Pound's poetry you have found in this book.

## LIBRARY EXERCISES

1. Compare the views of Robert Gorham Davis, David Rattray, and Allen Tate on the influence of the political ideas in Pound's verse. The Tate article (*Partisan Review*, XVI, 666-670) will be available in the library.

2. The so-called Hillyer controversy caused many articles and letters to be written. Using the bibliography provided at the end of this book, write a general account of this controversy.

3. What is the nature of Pound's monetary theories?

4. What does Pound himself say about his theories in Kunitz and Haycraft, *Twentieth Century Authors* (New York: The H. W. Wilson Company, 1942)?

5. What bibliographical items can you find that could be useful to someone attempting to write a paper about the influence of Pound on T. S. Eliot?

## TOPICS FOR LONG RESEARCH PAPERS

1. You have been asked to write a biography of Ezra Pound, in about 1500 words, for a newspaper obituary or an encyclopedia

article. Write as complete an account as the materials of this volume permit. Keep it *factual.*

2. You have been asked to write a factual account of The Bollingen Award of 1949, in about 1500 words, for a yearbook. Include an enumeration (with examples) of the various factions involved and positions taken during the controversy, but do *not* take issue or side with any.

3. William Barrett asked to put The Case as follows: "How far is it possible, in a lyric poem, for technical embellishments to transform vicious and ugly matter into beautiful poetry?" (*Partisan Review,* XVI, 347). Karl Shapiro chose to re-phrase this: "Through his experience with vicious and ugly ideas, what poetic insights into our world has this poet given us?" (*Ibid.,* 519.) Elect to answer one of these questions, in 1500-2500 words. Be scrupulous in citing sources that have influenced or are related to your findings.

4. Remember that (a) *The Pisan Cantos* was not the only volume of verse published in 1948, and that (b) the Fellows were under no obligation to make an award for that year. Look up and read the other 1948 volumes of verse by recognized poets. Does any seem as deserving as Pound's? Or would you have made no award at all? Explain and defend your stand in 2500 words.

## MORE AMBITIOUS TOPICS

Ezra Pound, the Poet as Exile
Pound's Beliefs vs. the Quality or Worth of His Poetry
Pound's Virtues and Limitations as a Cultural Critic
Government Sponsorship of the Arts: the Pound Case in Evidence
The Nature of Pound's Contribution to Modern Letters